On Relationship

Phyllis
Lane

September
1994

Other books by J. Krishnamurti from HarperCollins

The Awakening of Intelligence

Education and the Significance of Life

The Ending of Time (with David Bohm)

Exploration into Insight

The First and Last Freedom

The Flame of Attention

The Flight of the Eagle

Freedom from the Known

The Future of Humanity (with David Bohm)

Krishnamurti to Himself

Krishnamurti's Journal

Krishnamurti's Notebook

Life Ahead

Meeting Life

The Network of Thought

On Freedom

On Living and Dying

On Nature and the Environment

Truth and Actuality

The Wholeness of Life

On Relationship

J. Krishnamurti

HarperSanFrancisco

A Division of HarperCollinsPublishers

For additional information, write to:
Krishnamurti Foundation Trust, Ltd.
Brockwood Park, Bramdean, Hants, SO24 0LQ England

or

Krishnamurti Foundation of America
P.O. Box 1560
Ojai, CA 93023, United States

Sources and acknowledgments can be found on page 162.

Series editor: Mary Cadogan

Associate editors: Ray McCoy and David Skitt

FIRST EDITION

Library of Congress Cataloging-in-Publication Data

Krishnamurti, J. (Jiddu), 1895–1986

On relationship / J. Krishnamurti. — 1st ed.

p.   cm.

ISBN 0-06-250608-0 (alk. paper)

1. International relations.   I. Title.

HM132.K72   1992

302—dc20   91—55330

                                                            CIP

94   95   96   97   98   CWI   12   11   10   9   8   7   6   5   4   3   2

The problem is not the world, but you in relationship with another, which creates a problem; and that problem extended becomes the world problem.

Colombo
25 December 1949

Contents

Foreword

JIDDU KRISHNAMURTI was born in India in 1895 and, at the age of thirteen, was taken up by the Theosophical Society, which considered him to be the vehicle for the "world teacher" whose advent it had been proclaiming. Krishnamurti was soon to emerge as a powerful, uncompromising, and unclassifiable teacher, whose talks and writings were not linked to any specific religion and were of neither the East nor the West but for the whole world. Firmly repudiating the messianic image, in 1929 he dramatically dissolved the large and monied organization that had been built around him and declared truth to be "a pathless land," which could not be approached by any formalized religion, philosophy, or sect.

For the rest of his life Krishnamurti insistently rejected the guru status that others tried to foist upon him. He continued to attract large audiences throughout the world but claimed no authority, wanted no disciples, and spoke always as one individual to another. At the core of his teaching was the realization that fundamental changes in society can be brought about only by a transformation of individual consciousness. The need for self-knowledge and understanding of the restrictive, separative influences of religious and nationalistic conditionings was constantly stressed. Krishnamurti pointed always to the urgent need for openness, for that "vast space in the brain in which there is unimaginable energy." This seems to have been the wellspring of his own creativity and the key to his catalytic impact on such a wide variety of people.

He continued to speak all over the world until he died in 1986 at the age of ninety. His talks and dialogues, journals and letters have been collected into more than sixty books. From that vast body of teachings this series of theme books has been compiled. Each book focuses on an issue that has particular relevance to and urgency in our daily lives.

On Relationship

Ojai, 16 June 1940

FOR MOST OF US, relationship with another is based on dependence, either economic or psychological. This dependence creates
fear, breeds in us possessiveness, results in friction, suspicion, frustration. Economic dependence on another can perhaps be elimi-
nated through legislation and proper organization, but I am referring
especially to that psychological dependence on another, which is the
outcome of craving for personal satisfaction, happiness, and so on.
One feels, in this possessive relationship, enriched, creative, and
active; one feels one's own little flame of being is increased by another. In order not to lose this source of completeness, one fears
the loss of the other, and so possessive fears come into being with all
their resulting problems. Thus in this relationship of psychological
dependence, there must always be conscious or unconscious fear,
suspicion, that often lies hidden in pleasant-sounding words. The
reaction of this fear leads one ever to search for security and enrich-
ment through various channels, or to isolate oneself in ideas and ideals, or to seek substitutes for satisfaction.

Though one is dependent on another, there is yet the desire to be inviolate, to be whole. The complex problem in relationship is how to love without dependence, without friction and conflict; how to conquer the desire to isolate oneself, to withdraw from
the cause of conflict. If we depend for our happiness on another, on
society or on environment, they become essential to us; we cling to

them, and any alteration of these we violently oppose because we depend upon them for our psychological security and comfort. Though intellectually we may perceive that life is a continual process of flux, of mutation necessitating constant change, emotionally or sentimentally we cling to the established and comforting values; hence there is a constant battle between change and the desire for permanency. Is it possible to put an end to this conflict?

Life cannot be without relationship, but we have made it so agonizing and hideous by basing it on personal and possessive love. Can one love and yet not possess? You will find the true answer not in escape, ideals, beliefs but through the understanding of the causes of dependence and possessiveness. If one can deeply understand this problem of relationship between oneself and another then perhaps we shall understand and solve the problems of our relationship with society, for society is but the extension of ourselves. The environment that we call society is created by past generations; we accept it, as it helps us to maintain our greed, possessiveness, illusion. In this illusion there cannot be unity or peace. Mere economic unity brought about through compulsion and legislation cannot end war. As long as we do not understand individual relationship, we cannot have a peaceful society. Since our relationship is based on possessive love, we have to become aware, in ourselves, of its birth, its causes, its action. In becoming deeply aware of the process of possessiveness with its violence, fears, its reactions, there comes an understanding that is whole, complete. This understanding alone frees thought from dependence and possessiveness. It is within oneself that harmony in relationship can be found, not in another nor in environment.

In relationship, the primary cause of friction is oneself, the self that is the centre of unified craving. If we can but realize that it is not how another acts that is of primary importance, but how each one of us acts and reacts, and that if that reaction and action can be fundamentally, deeply understood, then relationship will undergo a deep and radical change. In this relationship with another, there is not only the physical problem but also that of thought and feeling on all levels, and one can be harmonious with another only when one is harmonious integrally in oneself. In relationship the important thing to bear in mind is not the other but oneself, which does not mean that one must isolate oneself, but understand deeply in oneself the cause of conflict and sorrow. So long as we depend on another for our psychological well-being, intellectually or emotionally, that dependence must inevitably create fear from which arises sorrow.

To understand the complexity of relationship there must be thoughtful patience and earnestness. Relationship is a process of self-revelation in which one discovers the hidden causes of sorrow. This self-revelation is only possible in relationship.

I am laying emphasis on relationship because in comprehending deeply its complexity we are creating understanding, an understanding that transcends reason and emotion. If we base our understanding merely on reason then there is isolation, pride, and lack of love in it, and if we base our understanding merely on emotion, then there is no depth in it; there is only a sentimentality that soon evaporates, and no love. From this understanding only can there be completeness of action. This understanding is impersonal and cannot be destroyed. It is no longer at the behest of time. If we cannot bring forth understanding from the everyday problems of greed and of our relationship, then to seek such understanding and love in other realms of consciousness is to live in ignorance and illusion.

Without fully understanding the process of greed, merely to cultivate kindliness, generosity, is to perpetuate ignorance and cruelty. Without integrally understanding relationship, merely to cultivate compassion, forgiveness, is to bring about self-isolation and to indulge in subtle forms of pride. In understanding craving fully, there is compassion, forgiveness. Cultivated virtues are not virtues. This understanding requires constant and alert awareness, a strenuousness that is pliable. Mere control with its peculiar training has its dangers, as it is one-sided, incomplete, and therefore shallow. Interest brings its own natural, spontaneous concentration in which there is the flowering of understanding. This interest is awakened by observing, questioning the actions and reactions of everyday existence.

To grasp the complex problem of life with its conflicts and sorrows, one must bring about integral understanding. This can be done only when we deeply comprehend the process of craving that is now the central force in our life.

Questioner: In speaking of self-revelation, do you mean revealing oneself to oneself or to others?

Krishnamurti: One often does reveal oneself to others, but what is important, to see yourself as you are or to reveal yourself to another? I have been trying to explain that if we allow it, all relationship acts as a mirror in which to perceive clearly that which is crooked and that which is straight. It gives the necessary focus to see sharply, but as I explained, if we are blinded by prejudice, opinions, beliefs, we cannot, however poignant relationship is, see clearly, without bias. Then relationship is not a process of self-revelation.

Our primary consideration is: What prevents us from perceiving truly? We are not able to perceive because our opinions about ourselves, our fears, ideals, beliefs, hopes, traditions, all act as veils. Without understanding the causes of these perversions we try to alter or hold on to what is perceived, and this creates further resistances and further sorrow. Our chief consideration should be, not to alter or to accept what is perceived, but to become aware of the many causes that bring about this perversion. Some may say that they have not the time to be aware, they are too occupied, and so on, but it is not a question of time but rather of interest. Then, in whatever they are occupied with, there is the beginning of awareness. To seek immediate results is to destroy the possibility of complete understanding.

Saanen, 31 July 1981

Questioner: If two people have a relationship of conflict and pain, can they resolve it, or must the relationship end? To have a good relationship isn't it necessary <u>for both to change</u>?

Krishnamurti: I hope the question is clear. What is the cause in relationship of pain, conflict, and all the problems that arise? What is the root of it? Please, in answering these questions, we are thinking together. I am not answering for you just to receive or accept or reject, but together we are inquiring into these questions. This is a question that concerns all human beings whether they are in the East, here, or in America. This is a problem that really concerns most human beings. Apparently two people, man and woman, cannot live together without conflict, without pain, without a sense of inequality, without that feeling that they are not profoundly related to each other. One asks why? There may be multiple causes: sex, temperament, opposite feelings, belief, ambition. There may be many, many causes for this lack of harmony in relationship. But what is really the source, the depth of that source, that brings conflict in each of us? I think that is the important question to ask, and then do not wait for an answer from somebody, like the speaker, but having put the question, have the patience to wait, hesitate, let the question itself take seed, flower, move. I don't know if I am conveying that feeling.

I ask myself why, if I am married to a woman, or live with a woman, why do I have this basic conflict between us? I can give a superficial answer—because she is a Roman Catholic and I am a Protestant, or this or that. Those are all superficial reasons, but I want to find out what is the deep root, or deep source of this conflict between two people. I have put the question, and I am waiting for the question itself to flower, to expose all the intricacies in the question and what the question brings out. For that, I must have a little patience—right?—a little sense of waiting, watching, being aware, so that the question begins to unfold. As it unfolds I begin to see the answer. Not that I want an answer, but the question itself begins to unroll, show me the extraordinary complexity that lies between two people, between two human beings that perhaps like each other, perhaps are attracted to each other. When they are very young they get sexually involved, and so on, and later as they grow a little older they get bored with each other and gradually escape from that boredom through another person, divorcing—you know all the rest of it. But they find the same problem with another. So I have to have patience. By that word *patience* I mean not allowing time to operate. I do not know if you have gone into the question of patience and impatience.

Most of us are rather impatient. We want our question answered immediately, or we want to escape from it immediately, to operate upon it immediately. So we are rather impatient to get on with it. This impatience doesn't give one the depth of understanding of the problem. Whereas if I have patience, which is not of time, I am not wanting to end the problem; I am watching, looking at the problem, letting it evolve, grow. So out of that patience I begin to find out the depth of the answer. Right? Let us do that together now. We are patient, not wanting an immediate answer, and therefore our minds, brains are open to look, are aware of the problem and its complexity. Right? We are trying—no, I don't want to use the word *trying*—we are penetrating into the problem of why two people can never seem to live together without conflict. What is the root of this conflict? What is my relationship with her, or with somebody? Is it superficial? That is, sexual attraction, the curiosity, the excitement, are all superficial sensory responses. Right? So I realize these responses are superficial, and as long as I try to find an answer superficially I will never be able to see the depth of the problem. So am I free from the superficial responses and the problems that superficial responses create and the attempt to solve those problems superficially? I don't know if you are following.

I have seen that I won't find an answer superficially. Therefore I ask what the root of it is. Is it education? Is it that being a man I want to dominate the other, that I want to possess the other? Am I attached so deeply I don't want to let go? And do I see that being tied, attached, will invariably bring about corruption—corruption in the sense that I am jealous, I am anxious, I am frightened? One knows very well all the consequences of attachment. Is that the cause of it? Or is the cause much deeper? First of all, we said, superficial, then emotional, attachment, emotional and sentimental and romantic dependence. If I discard those, then is there still a deeper issue involved in this? Are you getting it? We are moving from the superficial lower and deeper and deeper so that we can find out for ourselves what the root of it is. I hope you are doing this.

Now how do I find the root of it? How do you find the root of it? Are you wanting an answer, wanting to find the root of it and therefore making a tremendous effort? Or you want to find it so your mind, your brain is quiet? It is looking, so it is not agitated, it is not the activity of desire, will. It is just watching. Are we doing this together, just watching to see what is the deep root, or deep cause, the basis of this conflict between human beings? Is it the sense of individual separation? See, go into it very carefully please. Is it the individual concept that I am separate from the other basically? Biologically we are different, but there is the sense of deep-rooted individual separative action; is that the root of it? Or is there still a deeper root, a deeper layer—you understand? I wonder if you are following all this? We are together in this? First sensory responses, sensual responses, then emotional, romantic, sentimental responses, then attachment, with all its corruption? Or is it something profoundly conditioned, a brain that says, "I am an individual, and he, or she, is an individual, and we are separate entities; each must fulfil in his own way and therefore the separation is basic"? Is that so?

Is it basic? Or have I been educated to that, that I am an individual and she, also an individual, must fulfil herself in her own way, and I must equally? So we have already started from the very beginning in these two separate directions. They may be running parallel together but never meeting; like two railway lines that never meet. And all I am doing is trying to meet, trying to live harmoniously, struggling: "Oh, darling you are so good"—you follow?—repeating, repeating, but never meeting. Right?

So if that is the cause, and apparently it appears to be the cause, the root of it, is that separative existence of an individual a reality? Or it is an illusion that I have been nourishing, cherishing, holding onto, without any validity behind it? If it has no validity, I must be quite sure, absolutely, irrevocably sure that it is an illusion and ask if the brain can break away from that illusion and realize we are all similar, psychologically. You follow? My consciousness is the consciousness of the rest of mankind; though biologically we differ, psychologically, our consciousness is similar in all human beings. If I once realize this, not intellectually but in depth, in my heart, in my blood, in my guts, then my relationship to another undergoes a radical change. Right? It's inevitable.

Now the questioner asks: We are in conflict, must it end? If we battle with each other all day long, as most people do in this struggle, conflict—you know, the bitterness, the anger, the hatred, the repulsion—we bear it as long as we can and then comes the moment when we have to break. We know the familiar pattern of this. There are more and more divorces. And the questioner asks: What is one to do? If I am everlastingly in conflict with my wife and somehow I can't patch it over, must the relationship end? Or do I understand basically the cause of this disruption, of this conflict, which is the sense of separate individuality, and having seen the illusory nature of it, I am therefore no longer pursuing the individual line. So then what takes place when I have perceived that and live it—not verbally maintain it, but actually live it—what is my relationship with the person, with the woman who still thinks in terms of the individual? You understand my question?

It is very interesting. Go into it. I see, or she sees—better put it onto her—she sees the foolishness, the absurdity, the illusory nature of the individual. She understands it, she feels it, and I don't because I am a male, I am more aggressive, more driving, and all the rest of that. So what takes place between us? She has comprehended that nature and I have not. She won't quarrel with me, ever. Right? She won't enter into that area at all, but I am constantly pushing her, driving her and trying to pull her into that area. I am creating the conflict, not she. Have you understood how the whole thing has moved? Are you following all this? The whole thing has moved. There are now not two people quarrelling but only one. See what has taken place. And I, if I am at all sensitive, if I have real feeling for her, I begin to transform also because she is irrevocably there. You understand? She will not move out of that. See what happens. If two immovable objects meet there is conflict. I don't know if you see. But if one is immovable, the lady, and I am movable, I naturally yield to that which is immovable. Right? I wonder if you understand this. This is very simple.

So the problem then is resolved, if one has real comprehension of relationship—without the image, which we went into previously. Then by her very presence, by her very vitality of actuality, she is going to transform me, help me. That is the answer. Got it?

Bangalore, 15 August 1948

LIFE IS A process of constant movement in relationship, and without understanding relationship we shall bring about confusion and struggle and fruitless effort. So it is important to understand what we mean by relationship, because society is built out of relationship and there can be no isolation. There is no such thing as living in isolation. That which is isolated soon dies.

So our problem is what we mean by relationship. In understanding relationship, which is conduct between human beings whether intimate or distant, we shall begin to understand the whole process of existence and the conflict between bondage and independence. So we must very carefully examine what we mean by relationship. Is not relationship at present a process of isolation, and therefore a constant conflict? The relationship between you and another, between you and your wife, between you and society, is the product of this isolation. By isolation I mean that we are all the time seeking security, gratification, and power.

After all, each one of us in our relationship with another is seeking gratification; and where there is search for comfort, for security, whether it be in a nation or in an individual, there must be isolation, and that which is in isolation invites conflict. Any thing that resists is bound to produce conflict between itself and that which it is resisting; and since most of our relationship is a form of resistance, we create a society that inevitably breeds isolation and hence conflict within and without that isolation. So we must examine relationship as it actually works in our lives. What I am—my actions, my thoughts, my feelings, my motives, my intentions—brings about that relationship between myself and another, which we call society. There is no society without this relationship between two people; and before we can talk about national independence, wave the flag, and all the rest of it, we have to understand our relationship with one another.

Now if we examine our life, our relationship with another, we will see that it is a process of isolation. We are really not concerned with another; though we talk a great deal about it, actually we are not concerned. We are related to someone only as long as that relationship gratifies us, as long as it gives us a refuge, as long as it satisfies us. But the moment there is a disturbance in the relationship that produces discomfort in ourselves, we discard that relationship. In other words, there is relationship only as long as we are gratified. This may sound harsh, but if you really examine your life very closely, you will see it is a fact; and to avoid a fact is to live in ignorance, which can never produce right relationship.

So if we look into our lives and observe relationship, we see it is a process of building resistance against another, a wall over which we look and observe the other; but we always retain the wall and remain behind it, whether it be a psychological wall, a material wall, an economic wall, or a national wall. As long as we live in isolation, behind a wall, there is no relationship with another. We live enclosed because it is much more gratifying; we think it is much more secure. The world is so disruptive—there is so much sorrow, so much pain, war, destruction, misery—that we want to escape and live within the walls of security of our own psychological being. So relationship, with most of us, is actually a process of isolation, and obviously such relationship builds a society that is also isolating. That is exactly what is happening throughout the world. You remain in your isolation and stretch your hand over the wall, calling it internationalism, brotherhood, or what you will, but actually, sovereign governments, armies, continue. That is, clinging to your own limitations, you think you can create world unity, world peace, which is impossible. As long as you have a frontier, whether national, economic, religious, or social, it is an obvious fact that there cannot be peace in the world.

Now the process of isolation is a process of the search for power, and whether one is seeking power individually or for a racial or national group, there must be isolation, because the very desire for power, for position, is separatism. After all, that is what each one wants, is it not? He wants a powerful position in which he can dominate, whether at home, in the office, or in a bureaucratic regime. Each one is seeking power, and in seeking power he will establish a society that is based on power, military, industrial, economic, and so on—which again is obvious. Is not the desire for power in its very nature isolating? I think it is very important to understand this because the man who wants a peaceful world, a world in which there are no wars, no appalling destruction, no catastrophic misery on an immeasurable scale, must understand this fundamental question. As long as you, the individual, seek power, however much or however little, whether as a prime minister, as a governor, a lawyer, or merely as a husband or a wife in the home—that is, as long as you desire the sense of domination, the sense of compulsion, the sense of building power, influence—surely you are bound to create a society that is the result of an isolating process; because power in its very nature is isolating, is separating.

A man who is affectionate, who is kindly, has no sense of power, and therefore such a man is not bound to any nationality, to any flag. He has no flag. But the man who is seeking power in any form, whether derived from bureaucracy or from the self-projection that he calls God, is still caught in an isolating process. If you examine it very carefully, you will see that the desire for power in its very nature is a process of enclosure. Each one is seeking his own position, his own security, and as long as that motive exists, society must be built on an isolating process. Where there is the search for power, there is a process of isolation, and that which is isolated is bound to create conflict. That is exactly what is happening throughout the world. Each group is seeking power and thereby isolating itself.

This is the process of nationalism, of patriotism, ultimately leading to war and destruction.

Now, without relationship, there is no possibility of existence in life; and as long as relationship is based on power, on domination, there must be the process of isolation, which inevitably invites conflict. There is no such thing as living in isolation. No country, no people, no individual, can live in isolation; yet because you are seeking power in so many different ways, you breed isolation. The nationalist is a curse because through his very nationalistic, patriotic spirit, he is creating a wall of isolation. He is so identified with his country that he builds a wall against another. And what happens when you build a wall against something? That something is constantly beating against your wall. When you resist something, the very resistance indicates that you are in conflict with the other. So nationalism, which is a process of isolation, which is the outcome of the search for power, cannot bring about peace in the world. The man who is a nationalist and talks of brotherhood is telling a lie. He is living in a state of contradiction.

Peace in the world is essential; otherwise we will be destroyed. A few may escape, but there will be greater destruction than ever before unless we solve the problem of peace. Peace is not an ideal; an ideal is fictitious. What is actual must be understood, and that understanding of the actual is prevented by the fiction that we call an ideal. The actual is that each one is seeking power, titles, positions of authority, and so on, all of which is covered up in various forms by well-meaning words. This is a vital problem. It is not a theoretical problem nor one that can be postponed; it demands action now, because the catastrophe is obviously coming. If it does not come tomorrow, it will come next year, or soon after, because the momentum of the isolating process is already here; and he who really thinks about it must tackle the root of the problem, which is the individual's search for power, creating the power-seeking group, race, and nation.

Now, can one live in the world without the desire for power, for position, for authority? Obviously one can. One does it when one does not identify oneself with something greater. This identification with something greater—the party, the country, the race, the religion, God—is the search for power. Because you in yourself are empty, dull, weak, you like to identify yourself with something greater. That desire to identify yourself with something greater is the desire for power. That is why nationalism, or any communal spirit, is such a curse in the world; it is still the desire for power. So the important thing in understanding life, and therefore relationship, is to discover the motive that is driving each one of us; because what that motive is, the environment is. That motive brings either peace or destruction in the world. And so it is very important for each one of us to be aware that the world is in a state of misery and destruction, and to realize that if we are seeking power, consciously or unconsciously, we are contributing to that destruction, and therefore our relationship with society will be a constant process of conflict.

There are multiple forms of power; it is not merely the acquisition of position and wealth. The very desire to be something is a form of power, which brings isolation and therefore conflict. Unless each one understands the motive, the intention of his actions, mere government legislation is of very little importance, because the inner is always overcoming the outer. You may outwardly build a peaceful structure, but the men who run it will alter it according to their intention. That is why it is very important for those who wish to create a new culture, a new society, a new state, first to understand themselves. In becoming aware of oneself, of the various inward movements and fluctuations, one will understand the motives, the intentions, the perils that are hidden; and only in that awareness is there transformation. Regeneration can come about only when there is cessation of this search for power; and then only can we create a new culture, a society that will not be based on conflict, but on understanding. Relationship is a process of self-revelation, and without knowing oneself, the ways of one's own mind and heart, merely to establish an outward order, a system, a cunning formula, has very little meaning.

So what is important is to understand oneself in relationship with another. Then relationship becomes not a process of isolation, but a movement in which you discover your own motives, your own thoughts, your own pursuits; and that very discovery is the beginning of liberation, the beginning of transformation. It is only this immediate transformation that can bring about the fundamental, radical revolution in the world that is so essential. Revolution within the walls of isolation is not a revolution. Revolution comes only when the walls of isolation are destroyed, and that can take place only when you are no longer seeking power.

Ojai, 17 July 1949

I SUGGEST THAT we should be able to listen to what is being said without rejection or acceptance. We should be able to listen so that, if something new is being said, we do not immediately reject it. This does not mean that we must accept everything that is being said. That would be really absurd because then we would merely be building up authority, and where there is authority, there can be no thinking, feeling; there can be no discovery of the new. As most of us are inclined to accept something eagerly, without true understanding, there is a danger that we may accept without thought or investigation, without looking deeply into it. In this talk I may perhaps say something new, or put something differently, which you may pass by if you do not listen with that ease, with that quietness that brings understanding.

I want to discuss a subject that may be rather difficult: the question of action, activity, and relationship. But before I do that, we have to understand first what we mean by activity, what we mean by action. Because our whole life seems based on action, or rather, activity. I want to differentiate between activity and action. We seem to be so engrossed in doing things; we are so restless, so consumed with movement, doing something at any cost, getting on, achieving, striving for success. And what is the place of activity in relationship? Because life is a question of relationship. Nothing can exist in isolation, and if relationship is merely an activity, then relationship has not much significance. I do not know if you have noticed that the moment you cease to be active, there is immediately a feeling of nervous apprehension; you feel as though you are not alive, not alert, so you must keep going. And there is the fear of being alone, of going out for a walk alone, of being by yourself, without a book, without a radio, without talking; the fear of sitting quietly without doing something all the time with your hands or with your mind or with your heart.

So to understand activity, surely we must understand relationship, must we not? If we treat relationship as a distraction, as an escape from something else, relationship then is merely an activity. And is not most of our relationship merely a distraction, and therefore only a series of activities is involved in relationship? As I said, relationship has true significance only when it is a process of self-revelation, when it is revealing oneself in the very action of relationship. But most of us do not want to be revealed in relationship. On the contrary, we use relationship as a means of covering up our own insufficiency, our own troubles, our own uncertainty. So relationship becomes mere movement, mere activity. I do not know if you have noticed that relationship is very painful, and that as long as it is not a revealing process, in which you are discovering yourself, relationship is merely a means of escape from yourself.

I think it is important to understand this because the question of self-knowledge lies in the unfolding of relationship, whether to things, to people, or to ideas. Can relationship be based on an idea? Surely any act based on an idea must be merely the continuation of that idea, which is activity. Action is not based on an idea. Action is immediate, spontaneous, direct, without the process of thought involved. But when we base action on an idea, then it becomes an activity, and if we base our relationship on an idea, then surely such a relationship is merely an activity, without comprehension. It is merely carrying out a formula, a pattern, an idea. Because we want something out of relationship, such relationship is always restricting, limiting, confining.

Idea is the outcome of a want, of a desire, of a purpose. If I am related to you because I need you, physiologically or psychologically, then that relationship is obviously based on idea, because I want something from you. And such a relationship based on an idea cannot be a self-revealing process. It is merely a momentum, an activity, a monotony, in which habit is established. Hence, such relationship is always a strain, a pain, a contention, a struggle, causing us agony.

Is it possible to be related without idea, without demand, without ownership, possession? Can we commune with each other—which is real relationship on all the different levels of consciousness—if we are related to each other through a desire, a physical or psychological need? Can there be relationship without these conditioning causes arising from want? As I said, this is quite a difficult problem. One has to go very deeply and very quietly into it. It is not a question of accepting or rejecting.

We know what our relationship is at present—a contention, a struggle, a pain, or mere habit. If we can understand fully, completely, relationship with the one, then perhaps there is a possibility of understanding relationship with the many, that is, with society. If I do not understand my relationship with the one, I certainly shall not understand my relationship with the whole, with society, with the many. And if my relationship with the one is based on a need, on gratification, then my relationship with society must be the same. Therefore, there must follow contention, with the one and with the many. Is it possible to live, with the one and with the many, without demand? Surely, that is the problem—is it not?—not only between you and me, but between me and society. And to understand that problem, to inquire into it very deeply, you have to go into the question of self-knowledge, because without knowing yourself as you are, without knowing exactly "what is," you obviously cannot have right relationship with another. Do what you will—escape, worship, read, go to cinemas, turn on radios—as long as there is no understanding of yourself, you cannot have right relationship; hence the contention, battle, antagonism, confusion, not only in you, but outside of you and about you. As long as we use relationship merely as a means of gratification, of escape, as a distraction that is mere activity, there can be no self-knowledge. But self-knowledge is understood, is uncovered, its process is revealed, through relationship; that is, if you are willing to go into the question of relationship and expose yourself to it. Because, after all, you cannot live without relationship. But we want to use that relationship to be comfortable, to be gratified, to be something. That is, we use relationship based on an idea, which means the mind plays the important part in relationship. And as mind is concerned always with protecting itself, with remaining always within the known, it reduces all relationship to the level of habit, or of security; and therefore, relationship becomes merely an activity.

So you see that relationship, if we allow it, can be a process of self-revelation, but, since we do not allow it, relationship becomes merely a gratifying activity. As long as the mind merely uses relationship for its own security, that relationship is bound to create confusion and antagonism. Is it possible to live in relationship without the idea of demand, of want, of gratification?

YOU CANNOT THINK about love. You can think about the person whom you love, but that thought is not love, and so, gradually, thought takes the place of love. . . . Can relationship be based on an idea? If it is, is it not a self-enclosing activity and therefore isn't it inevitable that there should be contention, strife, and misery?

Rajahmundry, 4 December 1949

REALITY COMES INTO being only when the mind *is* still, not *made* still. Therefore, there must be no disciplining of the mind to be still. When you discipline yourself, it is merely a projected desire to be in a particular state. Such a state is not the state of passivity. Religion is the understanding of the thinker and the thought, which means the understanding of action in relationship. Such understanding is religion, not the worship of some idea, however gratifying, however traditional, whoever has said it. Religion is understanding the beauty, the depth, the extensive significance of action in relationship. Because, after all, life is relationship; to be, is to be related. Otherwise you have no existence. You cannot live in isolation. You are related to your friends, to your family, to those with whom you work. Even though you withdraw to a mountain, you are related to the man who brings food. You are related to an idea that you have projected. Existence implies being, which is relationship, and if we do not understand that relationship there is no understanding of reality. But because relationship is painful, disturbing, constantly changing in its demands, we escape from it to what we call God, which we think is the pursuit of reality. The pursuer cannot pursue the real. He can only pursue his own ideal, which is self-projected. So our relationship and the understanding of it is true religion and nothing else is, because in that relationship is contained the whole significance of existence. In relationship, whether with people, with nature, with the trees, with the stars, with ideas, with the State—in that relationship is the whole uncovering of the thinker and the thought, which is man, which is mind. The self comes into being through the focus of conflict; the focusing of conflict gives self-consciousness to the mind. Otherwise there is no self; and though you may place that self on a high level, it is still the self of gratification.

So the man who would receive reality, not seek reality, who would hear the voice of the eternal, whatever that eternal is, must understand relationship; because in relationship there is conflict, and it is that conflict which prevents the real. That is, in conflict there is the fixing of self-consciousness, which seeks to eschew, to escape conflict; but only when the mind understands conflict is it capable of receiving the real. So without understanding relationship, the pursuit of the real is the pursuit of an escape. Why not face it? Without understanding the actual, how can you go beyond? You may close your eyes, you may run away to shrines and worship empty images, but the worship, the devotion, the ritual, the giving of flowers, the sacrifices, the ideals, beliefs—all that has no meaning without understanding conflict in relationship. So the understanding of conflict in relationship is of primary importance, nothing else, for in that conflict you discover the whole process of the mind. Without knowing yourself as you are, not as you are technically supposed to be—God enclosed in matter, or whatever the theory is—but actually, in the conflict of daily existence—economic, social, and ideological—without understanding that conflict, how can you go beyond and find something? The search for the beyond is merely an escape from "what is," and if you want to escape, then religion or God is as good an escape as intoxication. Don't object to this putting drinking and God on the same level. All escapes are on the same level, whether you escape through drink, through church, or whatever it be.

So the understanding of conflict in relationship is of primary importance, and nothing else, because out of that conflict we create the world in which we live every day, the misery, the poverty, the ugliness of existence. Relationship is response to the movement of life. That is, life is a constant challenge, and when the response is inadequate, there is conflict; but to respond immediately, truly, adequately to the challenge, brings about a completeness. In that response which is adequate to the challenge there is the cessation of conflict. Therefore it is important to understand oneself, not in abstraction, but in actuality, in everyday existence. What you are in daily life is of the highest importance, not what you think about or what you have ideas about, but how you behave toward your wife, your husband, your children, your employees. Because, from what you are, you create the world. Conduct is not an ideal conduct. There is no ideal conduct. Conduct is what you are from moment to moment, how you behave from moment to moment. The ideal is an escape from what you are. How can you go far when you do not know what is near you, when you are not aware of your wife? Surely you must begin near to go far; but nevertheless your eyes are fixed on the horizon, which you call religion, and you have all the paraphernalia of belief to help you to escape.

So what is important is not how to escape, because any escape is as good as another; the religious escapes and the worldly escapes are all the same, and escapes do not solve our problem. Our problem is conflict, not only the conflict between individuals, but the world conflict. We see what is happening in the world, the increasing conflict of war, the destruction, the misery—that you cannot stop. All you can do is to alter your relationship with the world, not the world of Europe or America, but the world of your wife, your husband, your work, your home. There you can bring change, and that change moves in wider and wider circles; but without this fundamental change there can be no peace of mind. You may sit in a corner or read something to put yourself to sleep, which most people call meditation, but that is not the uncovering, the receiving of the real. What most of us want is a satisfying escape; we do not want to face our conflicts because they are too painful. They are painful only because we never look to see what they are all about; we seek something that we call God, but never look into the cause of conflict. But if we understand the conflict of everyday existence, then we can go further, because therein lies the whole significance of life. A mind that is in conflict is a destructive mind, a wasteful mind, and those in conflict can never understand; but conflict is not stilled by any sanctions, beliefs, or disciplines, because the conflict itself has to be understood. Our problem is in relationship, which is life; religion is the understanding of that life, which brings about a state in which the mind is quiet. Such a mind is capable of receiving the real. That, after all, is religion, not your church services, your rituals, your repetition of words, phrases, and ceremonies. Surely all that is not religion. Those are divisions, but a mind that is understanding relationship has no division. The belief that life is one is merely an idea and therefore has no value; but for a man who is understanding relationship there is no "outsider" or "insider," there is neither the foreigner nor the one who is near. Relationship is the process of understanding oneself, and to understand oneself from moment to moment in daily life is self-knowledge. Self-knowledge is not a religion, an ultimate end. There is no such thing as an ultimate end. There is such a thing for the man who wants to escape; but the understanding of relationship, in which there is ever-unfolding self-knowledge, is immeasurable.

So self-knowledge is not the knowledge of the self placed at some high level; it is from moment to moment in daily conduct, which is action, which is relationship; and without that self-knowledge there is no right thinking. You have no basis for right thinking if you do not know what you are. You cannot know yourself in abstraction, in ideology. You can know yourself only in relationship in your daily life. Don't you know that you are in conflict? What is the good of going away from it, of avoiding it, like a man who has a poison in his system that he does not reject and who is therefore slowly dying?

So self-knowledge is the beginning of wisdom, and without that self-knowledge you cannot go far. To seek the absolute, God, truth, or what you will, is merely the search for a self-projected gratification. Therefore, you must begin near and search every word that you speak, search every gesture, the way you talk, the way you act, the way you eat; be aware of everything without condemnation. Then in that awareness you will know what actually is and the transformation of what is, which is the beginning of liberation. Liberation is not an end. Liberation is from moment to moment in the understanding of what is, when the mind *is* free, not *made* free. It is only a free mind that can discover, not a mind moulded by a belief or shaped according to a hypothesis. Such a mind cannot discover. There can be no freedom if there is conflict, for conflict is the fixing of the self in relationship.

Colombo, 25 December 1949

SURELY INCREASING CONFUSION arises because we approach a problem with a pattern of action, with an ideology, whether political or religious. Organized religion obviously prevents the understanding of a problem because the mind is conditioned by dogma and belief. Our difficulty is how to understand a problem directly, not through any particular religious or political conditioning; how to understand the problem so that the conflict may cease, not temporarily but completely, so that man can live fully, without the misery of tomorrow or the burden of yesterday. Surely that is what we must find out— how to meet the problem anew—because every problem, whether political, economic, religious, social, or personal, is ever new, and it cannot be met with the old. Perhaps this is putting it in a way different from that to which you are accustomed, but it is actually the issue. After all, life is a constantly changing environment.

We would like to sit back and be comfortable. We would like to shelter ourselves in religion and belief, or in knowledge based on particular facts. We would like to be comfortable, we would like to be gratified, we would like not to be disturbed; but life, which is ever changing, ever new, is always disturbing to the old. So our question is how to meet the challenge afresh. We are the result of the past; our thought is the outcome of yesterday, and with yesterday we obviously cannot meet today, because today is new. When we approach the new with yesterday, we are continuing the conditioning of yesterday in understanding today. So our problem in approaching the new is how to understand the old, and therefore be free of the old. The old cannot understand the new; you cannot "put new wine into old bottles." So it is important to understand the old, which is the past, which is the mind based on thinking.

Thought, idea, is the outcome of the past. Whether it is historical or scientific knowledge, or mere prejudice and superstition, idea is obviously the outcome of the past. We would not be able to think if we had no memory. Memory is the residue of experience, memory is the response of thought. To understand the challenge, which is new, we have to understand the total process of the self, which is the outcome of our past, the outcome of our conditioning—environmentally, socially, climatically, politically, economically—the whole structure of ourselves. To understand the problem is to understand ourselves. The understanding of the world begins with the understanding of ourselves. The problem is not the world, but you in relationship with another, which creates a problem; and that problem extended becomes the world problem.

So to understand this enormous, complex machine, this conflict, pain, confusion, misery, we must begin with ourselves, but not individualistically, in opposition to the mass. There is no such thing as that abstraction called the mass; but when you and I do not understand ourselves, when we follow a leader and are hypnotized by words, then we become the mass and are exploited. So the solution to the problem is not to be found in isolation, in withdrawal to a monastery, to a mountain or a cave, but in understanding the whole problem of ourselves in relationship. You cannot live in isolation; to be is to be related. So our problem is relationship, which causes conflict, which brings misery, constant trouble. As long as we do not understand that relationship, it will be a source of endless pain and struggle. Understanding ourselves, which is self-knowledge, is the beginning of wisdom; and for self-knowledge you cannot go to a book. There is no book that can teach it to you. Know yourself, and once you understand yourself, you can deal with the problems that confront each one of us every day. Self-knowledge brings tranquillity to the mind, and then only can truth come into being. Truth cannot be sought after. Truth is the unknown, and that which you seek is already known. Truth comes into being unsought when the mind is without prejudice, when there is the understanding of the whole process of ourselves.

Colombo, 28 December 1949

SELF-KNOWLEDGE IS NOT a thing to be bought in books, nor is it the outcome of a long painful practise and discipline. It is awareness, from moment to moment, of every thought and feeling as it arises in relationship. Relationship is not on an abstract ideological level, but is an actuality, the relationship with property, with people and with ideas. Relationship implies existence; and as nothing can live in isolation, to be is to be related. Our conflict is in relationship, at all the levels of our existence; and the understanding of this relationship, completely and extensively, is the only real problem that each one has. This problem cannot be postponed or evaded. The avoidance of it only creates further conflict and misery. The escape from it only brings about thoughtlessness, which is exploited by the crafty and the ambitious.

Religion then is not belief, nor dogma, but the understanding of truth that is to be discovered in relationship, from moment to moment. Religion that is belief and dogma is only an escape from the reality of relationship. The man who seeks God, or what you will, through belief that he calls religion, only creates opposition, bringing about separation that is disintegration. Any form of ideology, whether of the right or of the left, of this particular religion or of that, sets man against man, which is what is happening in the world.

The replacement of one ideology by another is not the solution to our problems. The problem is not which is the better ideology, but the understanding of ourselves as a total process. You might say that the understanding of ourselves takes infinite time and in the meanwhile the world is going to pieces. You think that if you have a planned action according to an ideology, then there is a possibility of bringing about, soon, a transformation in the world. If we look a little more closely into this, we will see that ideas do not bring people together at all. An idea may help to form a group, but that group is against another with a different idea and so on until ideas become more important than action: ideologies, beliefs, organized religions, separate people.

THE EXPERIENCE OF another is not valid for the understanding of reality. But the organized religions throughout the world are based on the experience of another and, therefore, are not liberating man but only binding him to a particular pattern that sets man against man. Each one of us has to start anew, afresh, for what *we* are, the world is. The world is not different from you and me. This little world of our problems, extended, becomes the world and the problems of the world.

We despair of our understanding in relation to the vast problems of the world. We do not see that it is not a problem of mass action, but of the awakening of the individual to the world in which he lives, and to resolve the problems of his world, however limited. The mass is an abstraction that is exploited by the politician, by one who has an ideology. The mass is actually you and I and another. When you and I and another are hypnotized by a word, then we become the mass, which is still an abstraction, for the word is an abstraction. Mass action is an illusion. This action is really the idea about an action of the few that we accept in our confusion and despair. Out of our confusion and despair, we choose our guides, either political or religious, and they must inevitably, because of our choice, also be in confusion and despair. They may put on an air of certainty and all-knowingness, but actually, as they are the guides of the confused, they must be equally confused, or they would not be guides. In the world where the leader and the led are confused, to follow a pattern or an ideology, knowingly or unknowingly, is to breed further conflict and misery.

❖

THE WORLD IS your problem and to comprehend it you must understand yourself. This understanding of yourself is not a matter of time. You exist only in relationship; otherwise you are not. Your relationship is the problem, your relationship to property, to people and to ideas, or to beliefs. This relationship is now friction, conflict, and so long as you do not understand your relationship, do what you will, hypnotize yourself by any ideology or dogma, there can be no rest for you. This understanding of yourself is action in relationship. You discover yourself as you are directly in relationship. Relationship is the mirror in which you can see yourself as you are. You cannot see yourself as you are in this mirror if you approach it with a conclusion and an explanation, or with condemnation, or with justification.

The very perception of what you are, as you are, in the moment of action in relationship, brings a freedom from "what is." Only in freedom can there be discovery. A conditioned mind cannot discover truth. Freedom is not an abstraction; it comes into being with virtue. For the very nature of virtue is to bring liberation from the causes of confusion. After all, non-virtue is disorder, conflict. But virtue is freedom, the clarity of perception that understanding brings. You cannot become virtuous. The becoming is the illusion of greed, or acquisitiveness. Virtue is the immediate perception of "what is." So self-knowledge is the beginning of wisdom, and it is wisdom that will resolve your problems and so the problems of the world.

Colombo, 1 January 1950

IT IS IMPORTANT, before we ask what to do or how to act, to discover what right thinking is, because without right thinking, obviously there cannot be right action. Action according to a pattern, according to a belief, has set man against man. There can be no right thinking as long as there is no self-knowledge, because without self-knowledge, how can one know what one is actually thinking? We do a great deal of thinking, and there is a great deal of activity, but such thought and action produce conflict and antagonism, which we see not only in ourselves, but also about us in the world. So our problem is how to think rightly, which will produce right action, thereby eliminating the conflict and confusion that we find not only in ourselves, but in the world about us.

IF OUR THOUGHT is based on the background that is our conditioning, whatever we think is obviously merely a reaction and therefore leads to further conflict. So before we can find out what right thinking is, we have to know what self-knowledge is. Self-knowledge, surely, is not merely learning a particular kind of thinking. Self-knowledge is not based on ideas, belief, or conclusion. It must be a living thing, otherwise it ceases to be self-knowledge and becomes mere information. There is a difference between information, which is knowledge, and wisdom, which is knowing the processes of our thoughts and feelings. But most of us are caught up in information, superficial knowledge, and so we are incapable of going much deeper into the problem. To discover the whole process of self-knowledge we have to be aware in relationship. Relationship is the only mirror we have, a mirror that will not distort, a mirror in which we can exactly and precisely see our thought unfolding itself. Isolation, which many people seek, is the surreptitious building up of resistance against relationship. Isolation obviously prevents the understanding of relationship, relationship with people, with ideas, with things. As long as we don't know what the relationship actually is between ourselves and our property, ourselves and people, ourselves and ideas, obviously there must be confusion and conflict.

So we can find out what is right thinking only in relationship. That is, we can discover in relationship how we think from moment to moment, what our reactions are, and thereby proceed step by step to the unfoldment of right thinking. This is not an abstract or difficult thing to do, to watch exactly what is taking place in our relationship, what our reactions are, and thus discover the truth of each thought, each feeling. But if we bring to it an idea or a preconception of what relationship should be, then obviously that prevents the uncovering, the unfoldment of "what is." That is our difficulty; we have already made up our minds as to what relationship should be. To most of us, relationship is a term for comfort, for gratification, for security, and in that relationship we use property, ideas, and persons for our gratification. We use belief as a means of security. Relationship is not merely a mechanical adjustment. When we use people, it necessitates possession, physical or psychological, and in possessing someone we create all the problems of jealousy, envy, loneliness, and conflict. If we examine it a little more closely and deeply, we will see that using a person or property for gratification is a process of isolation. This process of isolation is not actual relationship at all. So our difficulty and our mounting problems come with the lack of understanding of relationship, which is essentially self-knowledge. If we do not know how we are related to people, to property, to ideas, then our relationship will inevitably bring about conflict. That is our whole problem at the present time, is it not?—relationship not only between people, but between groups of people, between nations, between ideologies, either of the left or of the right, religious or secular. Therefore, it is important to understand fundamentally your relationship with your wife, with your husband, with your neighbour; for relationship is a door through which we can discover ourselves, and through that discovery we understand what is right thinking.

Right thinking, surely, is entirely different from right thought. Right thought is static. You can learn about right thought, but you cannot learn about right thinking, because right thinking is movement, it is not static. Right thought you can learn from a book, from a teacher, or gather information about, but you cannot have right thinking by following a pattern or a mould. Right thinking is the understanding of relationship from moment to moment, which uncovers the whole process of the self.

At whatever level you live, there is conflict, not only individual conflict, but also world conflict. The world is you; it is not separate from you. What you are, the world is. There must be a fundamental revolution in your relationship with people, with ideas. There must be a fundamental change, and that change must begin, not outside you, but in your relationships. Therefore, it is essential for a man of peace, for a man of thought, to understand himself. For without self-knowledge his efforts only create further confusion and further misery. Be aware of the total process of yourself. You need no guru, no book, to understand from moment to moment your relationship with all things.

Questioner: Why do you waste your time preaching instead of helping the world in a practical way?

Krishnamurti: Now, what do you mean by *practical?* You mean bringing about a change in the world, a better economic adjustment, a better distribution of wealth, a better relationship, or to put it more brutally, helping you to find a better job. You want to see a change in the world, every intelligent man does, and you want a method to bring about that change, and therefore you ask me why I waste my time preaching instead of doing something about it. Now, is what I am actually doing a waste of time? It would be a waste of time, if I introduced a new set of ideas to replace the old ideology, the old pattern. Perhaps that is what you want me to do. But instead of pointing out a so-called practical way to act, to live, to get a better job, to create a better world, is it not important to find out what the impediments are that actually prevent a real revolution, not a revolution of the left or the right, but a fundamental, radical revolution, not based on ideas? Because ideals, beliefs, ideologies, dogmas, prevent action. There cannot be a world transformation, a revolution, as long as action is based on ideas, because action then is merely reaction in which ideas become much more important than action. That is precisely what is taking place in the world, isn't it? To act, we must discover the impediments that prevent action. But most of us don't want to act, that is our difficulty. We prefer to discuss, we prefer to substitute one ideology for another, and so we escape from action through ideology. Surely that is very simple, is it not? The world at the present time is facing many problems: overpopulation, starvation, division of people into nationalities and classes, and so on. Why isn't there a group of people sitting together trying to solve the problems of nationalism? But if we try to become international while clinging to our nationality, we create another problem; and that is what most of us do.

So you see that it is ideals which are really preventing action. A statesman, an eminent authority, has said the world can be organized and all the people fed. Then why is it not done? Because of conflicting ideas, beliefs, and nationalism. Therefore, ideas are actually preventing the feeding of people; and most of us play with ideas and think we are tremendous revolutionaries, hypnotizing ourselves with such words as *practical*. What is important is to free ourselves from ideas, from nationalism, from all religious beliefs and dogmas, so that we can act, not according to a pattern or an ideology, but as needs demand. Surely to point out the hindrances and impediments that prevent such action is not a waste of time, is not a lot of hot air. What you are doing is obviously nonsense. Your ideas and beliefs, your political, economic, and religious panaceas, are actually dividing people and leading to war. It is only when the mind is free of idea and belief that it can act rightly. A man who is patriotic, nationalistic, can never know what it is to be brotherly, though he may talk about it; on the contrary, his actions, economically and in every direction, are conducive to war. So there can be right action and therefore radical, lasting transformation, only when the mind is free of ideas, not superficially, but fundamentally; and freedom from ideas can take place only through self-awareness and self-knowledge.

Colombo, 8 January 1950

ONE OF OUR major problems is the question of creative living. Obviously, most of us have dull lives. We have only a very superficial reaction; most of our responses are superficial and thereby create innumerable problems. Creative living does not necessarily mean becoming a big architect or a great writer. That is merely capacity, and capacity is entirely different from creative living. No one need know that you are creative, but you yourself can know that state of extraordinary happiness, a quality of indestructibility. But that is not easily realized, because most of us have innumerable problems—political, social, economic, religious, family—that we try to solve according to certain explanations, certain rules, traditions, any sociological or religious pattern with which we are familiar. But our solution of one problem seems inevitably to create other problems, and we set up a net of problems ever multiplying and increasing in their destructiveness.

When we try to find a way out of this mess, this confusion, we seek the answer at one particular level. One must have the capacity to go beyond all levels, because the creative way of living cannot be found at any particular level. That creative action comes into being only in understanding relationship, and relationship is communion with another. So it is not really a selfish outlook to be concerned with individual action. We seem to think that we can do very little in this world, that only the big politicians, the famous writers, the great religious leaders, are capable of extraordinary action.

Actually, you and I are infinitely more capable of bringing about a radical transformation than the professional politicians and economists. If we are concerned with our own lives, if we understand our relationship with others, we will have created a new society; otherwise, we will but perpetuate the present chaotic mess and confusion.

So it is not out of selfishness, not because of a desire for power, that one is concerned with individual action. If we can find a way of living that is creative, not merely conforming to religious, social, political, or economic standards as we are doing at the present time, then I think we will be able to solve our many problems. At present we are merely repetitive gramophones, perhaps changing records occasionally under pressure, but most of us always play the same tunes for every occasion. It is this constant repetition, this perpetuation of tradition, that is the source of the problem with all its complexities. We seem to be incapable of breaking away from conformity, though we may substitute a new conformity for the present one, or try to modify the present pattern. It is a constant process of repetition, imitation. We are Buddhists, Christians, or Hindus; we belong to the left or to the right. By quoting from the various sacred books, by mere repetition, we think we shall solve our innumerable problems. Surely repetition is not going to solve human problems. What has the "revolutionary" done for the so-called masses? Actually, the problems are still there. What happens is that this constant repetition of an idea prevents the understanding of the problem itself. Through self-knowledge one has the capacity to free oneself from this repetition. Then it is possible to be in that creative state which is always new, and therefore one is always ready to meet each problem afresh. After all, our difficulty is that, having these immense problems, we meet them with previous conclusions, with the record of experience, either our own or acquired through others; and so we meet the new with the old, which creates a further problem.

Creative living is being without that background; the new is met as the new, therefore it does not create further problems.

Therefore it is necessary to meet the new with the new until we can understand the total process, the whole problem of mounting disaster, misery, starvation, war, unemployment, inequality, the battle between conflicting ideologies. That struggle and confusion is not to be solved by repetition of old ways. If you will really look a little more closely, without prejudice, without religious bias, you will see much bigger problems; and being free from conformity, from belief, you will be able to meet the new. This capacity to meet the new with the new is called the creative state, and that surely is the highest form of religion. Religion is not merely belief, it is not the following of certain rituals, dogmas, calling yourself this or that. Religion is really experiencing a state in which there is creation. This is not an idea, a process. It can be realized when there is freedom from self. There can be freedom from self only through understanding the self in relationship; but there can be no understanding in isolation.

As I have suggested, it is important that we experience each question as it arises, and not merely listen to my answers, that we discover together the truth of the matter, which is much more difficult. Most of us would like to be apart from the problem, watching others; but if we can discover together, take the journey together, so that it is your experience and not mine—though you are listening to my words if we can go together, then it will be of lasting value and importance.

Questioner: Do you advocate vegetarianism? Would you object to the inclusion of an egg in your diet?

Krishnamurti: Is that really a very great problem, whether we should have an egg or not? Perhaps most of you are concerned with non-killing. What is really the crux of the matter? Perhaps most of you eat meat or fish. You avoid killing by going to a butcher, or you put the blame on the killer, the butcher; that is only dodging the problem. If you like to eat eggs, you may get infertile eggs to avoid killing. But this is a very superficial question; the problem is much deeper. You don't want to kill animals for your stomach, but you do not mind supporting governments that are organized to kill. All sovereign governments are based on violence, they must have armies, navies, and air forces. You don't mind supporting them, but you object to the terrible calamity of eating an egg. See how ridiculous the whole thing is! Investigate the mentality of the gentleman who is nationalistic, who does not mind the exploitation and the ruthless destruction of people, to whom wholesale massacre is nothing—but who has scruples as to what goes into his mouth.

There is much more involved in this problem, not only the whole question of killing, but the right employment of the mind. The mind may be used narrowly, or it is capable of extraordinary activity. Most of us are satisfied with superficial activity, with security, sexual satisfaction, amusement, religious belief; with that we are satisfied and discard entirely the deeper response and wider significance of life. Even the religious leaders have become petty in their response to life. After all, the problem is not only killing animals but human beings, which is more important. You may refrain from using animals and degrading them, you may be compassionate about killing them, but what is important in this question is the whole problem of exploitation and killing, not only the slaughter of human beings in wartime, but the way you exploit people, the way you treat others, and look down on them as inferiors. Probably you are not paying attention to this, because it is near home. You would rather discuss God or reincarnation—but nothing that requires immediate action and responsibility.

Colombo, 22 January 1950, Public Talk

WHAT IS IMPORTANT is how we approach any problem. It is essential that we see very clearly that it is the lack of right relationship that brings about conflict, and it is therefore essential that we understand conflict in relationship, the whole process of our thought and action. Obviously, if we do not understand ourselves in relationship, whatever society we create, whatever ideas, opinions we may have, will only bring about further mischief and further misery. Therefore, the understanding of the whole process of oneself in relationship with society is the first step in understanding the problem of conflict. Self-knowledge is the beginning of wisdom, because you are the world, you are not separate from the world. Society is your relationship with another; you have created it, and the solution lies through your own understanding of that relationship, the interaction between you and society. Without understanding yourself, to seek a solution is utterly useless; it is merely an escape. What is important is understanding relationship. It is relationship that causes conflict, and that relationship cannot be understood unless we have the capacity to be passively watchful. Then, in that passive alertness, in that awareness, there comes understanding.

Questioner: I find that loneliness is the underlying cause of many of my problems. How can I deal with it?

Krishnamurti: What do you mean by loneliness? Are you actually aware that you are lonely? Surely loneliness is not a state of aloneness. Very few of us are alone; we don't want to be alone. It is essential to understand that aloneness is not isolation. There is a difference between being alone and isolation. Isolation is the sense of being enclosed, the sense of having no relationships, a feeling that you have been cut off from everything. That is entirely different from being alone, which is to be extraordinarily vulnerable. When we are lonely, a feeling of fear, anxiety, the ache of finding oneself in isolation, comes over one. When you love somebody, you feel that without that somebody you are lost. That person becomes essential to you in order for you not to feel the sense of isolation. So you use the person in order to escape from what you are. That is why we try to establish relationship, a communion with another, or establish a contact with things, property, just so that we feel alive. We acquire furniture, dresses, cars; we seek to accumulate knowledge, or become addicted to love.

By loneliness we mean that state which comes upon the mind, a state of isolation, a state in which there is no contact, no relationship, no communion with anything. We are afraid of it, we call it painful; and being afraid of what we are, of our actual state, we run away from it, using so many ways of escape—God, drink, the radio, amusements—anything to get away from that sense of isolation. Are not our actions, both in individual relationship and in relationship with society, an isolating process? Is not the relationship of father, mother, wife, husband, an isolating process for us at the present time? Is not that relationship almost always a relationship based on mutual need? So the process of self-isolation is simple—you are all the time seeking, in your relationships, an advantage for yourself. This isolating process is going on continually, and when awareness of isolation comes upon us through our own activities, we want to run away from it. So we go to the temple, or back to a book, or turn on the radio, or sit in front of a picture and meditate—anything to get away from what is.

Colombo, 22 January 1950, Radio Talk

ACTION HAS MEANING only in relationship and without understanding relationship, action on any level will only breed conflict. The understanding of relationship is infinitely more important than the search for any plan of action. The ideology, the pattern for action, prevents action. Action based on ideology hinders the understanding of relationship between man and man. Ideology may be of the right or of the left, religious or secular, but it is invariably destructive of relationship. The understanding of relationship is true action. Without understanding relationship, strife and antagonism, war and confusion are inevitable.

Relationship means contact, communion. There cannot be communion where people are divided by ideas. A belief may gather a group of people around itself. Such a group will inevitably breed opposition and so form another group with a different belief.

Ideas postpone direct relationship with the problem. It is only when there is direct relationship with the problem that there is action. But unfortunately, all of us approach a problem with conclusions, with explanations, which we call ideas. They are the means of postponing action. Idea is thought verbalized. Without the word, the symbol, the image, thought is not. Thought is the response of memory, of experience, which are the conditioning influences. These influences are not only of the past, but of the past in conjunction with the present. So the past is always shadowing the present. Idea is the response of the past to the present, and so idea is always limited, however extensive it may be. So ideas must always separate people.

The world is always close to catastrophe, but it seems to be closer now. Seeing approaching catastrophe, most of us take shelter in ideas. We think that *this* catastrophe, *this* crisis, can be solved by an ideology. Ideology is always an impediment to direct relationship and prevents action. We want peace only as an idea, not as an actuality. We want peace on the verbal level, which is only on the thinking level although we proudly call it the intellectual level. But the word *peace* is not peace. Peace can only be when the confusion that you and another make ceases. We are attached to the world of ideas and not to peace. We search for new social and political patterns and not for peace. We are concerned with the reconciliation of effects and not in putting aside the cause of war. This search will bring only answers conditioned by the past. This conditioning is what we call knowledge, experience, and the new changing facts are translated, interpreted, according to this knowledge. So there is conflict between what is and the experience that has been. The past, which is knowledge, must ever be in conflict with the fact, which is ever in the present. So this will not solve the problem but will perpetuate the conditions that have created the problem.

RELATIONSHIP IS OUR problem, not at any one particular level but at all the levels of our existence. This is the only problem we have. To understand relationship, we must come to it with freedom from all ideology, from all prejudice, not merely from the prejudice of the uneducated but also from the prejudice of knowledge. There is no such thing as understanding the problem from past experience. Each problem is new. There is no such thing as an old problem. When we approach a problem, which is always new, with an idea that is invariably the outcome of the past, our response is also of the past, which prevents understanding the problem.

The search for an answer to the problem only intensifies it. The answer is not away from it but only in the problem itself. We must see the problem afresh and not through the screen of the past. The inadequacy of response to challenge creates the problem. This inadequacy has to be understood and not the challenge. We are eager to see the new, and we cannot see it because the image of the past prevents the clear perception of it. We respond to challenge only as Catholics, Hindus, or Buddhists, or as of the left or of the right, and this invariably produces further conflict. So what is important is not seeing the new but the removal of the old. When the response is adequate to the challenge then only is there no conflict, no problem. This has to be seen in our daily life and not in the newspapers.

Relationship is the challenge of everyday life. If you and I and another do not know how to meet each other, we are creating conditions that breed war. So the world problem is your problem. You are not different from the world. The world is you. What you are, the world is. You can save the world, which is yourself, only in understanding the relationship of your daily life, not through belief called religion, or the left or the right, or through any reform, however extensive. The hope is not in the expert, in the ideology, or in the new leader. It lies in you.

You might ask how you, living an ordinary life in a limited circle, could affect the present world crisis. You do not think you will be able to. The present struggle is the outcome of the past that you and another have created. Until you and another radically alter the present relationship, you will only contribute to further misery. This is not oversimplification. If you go into it fully, you will see how your relationship with another, when extended, brings about world conflict and antagonism.

The world is you. Without the transformation of the individual which is you, there can be no radical revolution in the world. The revolution in social order without the individual transformation will lead only to further conflict and disaster. For society is the relationship of you and me and another. Without radical revolution in this relationship, all effort to bring peace is only a reformation, however revolutionary, which is retrogression.

Relationship based on mutual need brings only conflict. However interdependent we are on each other, we are using each other for a purpose, for an end. With an end in view, relationship is not. You may use me and I may use you. In this usage, we lose contact. A society based on mutual usage is the foundation of violence. When we use another, we have only the picture of the end to be gained. The end, the gain, prevents relationship, communion. In the usage of another, however gratifying and comforting it may be, there is always fear. To avoid this fear, we must possess. From this possession there arises envy, suspicion, and constant conflict. Such a relationship can never bring about happiness.

A society whose structure is based on mere need, whether physiological or psychological, must breed conflict, confusion, and misery. Society is the projection of yourself in relation with another, in which the need and the use are predominant. When you use another for your need, physically or psychologically, in actuality there is no relationship at all; you really have no contact with the other, no communion with the other. How can you have communion with the other, when the other is used as a piece of furniture, for your convenience and comfort? So it is essential to understand the significance of relationship in daily life.

We do not understand relationship; the total process of our being, our thought, our activity, makes for isolation that prevents relationship. The ambitious, the crafty, the believer, can have no relationship with another. He can only use another, which makes for confusion and enmity. This confusion and enmity exist in our present social structure; they will exist also in any reformed society as long as there is no fundamental revolution in our attitude towards another human being. As long as we use another as a means towards an end, however noble, there will inevitably be violence and disorder.

If you and I bring about fundamental revolution in ourselves not based on mutual need, either physical or psychological, then has not our relationship to the other undergone a fundamental transformation? Our difficulty is that we have a picture of what the new organized society should be and we try to fit ourselves into that pattern. The pattern is obviously fictitious. But what is real is that which we actually are, in the understanding of what we are, which is seen clearly in the mirror of daily relationship. To follow the pattern only brings about further conflict and confusion.

The present social disorder and misery must work itself out. But you and I and another can and must see the truth of relationship and so start a new action that is not based on mutual need and gratification. Mere reformation of the present structure of society, without altering fundamentally our relationship, is retrogression. A revolution that maintains the usage of man towards an end, however promising, is productive of further wars and untold sorrow. The end is always the projection of our own conditioning. However promising and utopian it might be, the end can only be a means of further confusion and pain. What is important in all this is not the new patterns, the new superficial changes, but the understanding of the total process of man, which is yourself.

In the process of understanding yourself, not in isolation but in relationship, you will find that there is a deep, lasting transformation in which the usage of another as a means for your own psychological gratification has come to an end. What is important is not how to act, what pattern to follow, or which ideology is the best, but the understanding of your relationship with another. This understanding is the only revolution, and not the revolution based on idea. Any revolution based on an ideology maintains man as a means only.

As the inner always overcomes the outer, without understanding the total psychological process, which is yourself, there is no basis for thinking at all. Any thought that produces a pattern of action will only lead to further ignorance and confusion.

There is only one fundamental revolution. This revolution comes into being when the need for using another ceases. This transformation is not an abstraction, a thing to be wished for, but an actuality that can be experienced, as we begin to understand the way of our relationship. This fundamental revolution may be called love; it is the only creative factor in bringing about transformation in ourselves and so in society.

Bombay, 9 March 1955

Questioner: How can I be free from fear?

Krishnamurti: What is fear? Fear exists only in relationship to something, it does not exist by itself. Fear comes into being in relationship to an idea, to a person, with regard to the loss of property, and so on. One may be afraid of death, which is the unknown. There is fear of public opinion, of what people will say, fear of losing a job, fear of being scolded or nagged. There are various forms of fear, deep and superficial, but all fear is in relationship to something. So when we ask, "Can I be free from fear?" it really means, "Can I be free from all relationship?" Do you understand? If it is relationship that is causing fear, then to ask if one can be free from fear is like asking if one can live in isolation. Obviously no human being can do that. There is no such thing as living in isolation, one can live only in relationship. So to be free from fear one must understand relationship, the relationship of the mind to its own ideas, to certain values, the relationship between husband and wife, between man and his property, between man and society. If I can understand my relationship with you, then there is no fear, because fear does not exist by itself, it is self-created in relationship. Our problem, then, is not how to overcome fear, but to find out first of all what our relationship is now, and what right relationship is. We do not have to establish right relationship, because in the very understanding of relationship, right relationship comes into being.

I think it is important to see that nothing can live in isolation. Even though you may become a monk or hermit, put on a loincloth and seclude yourself, isolate yourself in a belief, no human being can live in isolation. But the mind is pursuing isolation in the self-enclosure of "my experience," "my belief," "my wife," "my husband," "my property," which is a process of exclusion. The mind is seeking isolation in all its relationships, and hence there is fear. So our problem is to understand relationship.

Now what is relationship? When you say, "I am related," what does that mean? Apart from the purely physical relationship through contact, through blood, through heredity, our relationship is based on ideas, is it not? We are examining what is, not what should be. Our relationship at present is based on ideas, on ideation as to what we think is relationship. That is, our relationship with everything is a state of dependency. I believe in a certain idea because that belief gives me comfort, security, a sense of wellbeing; it acts as a means of disciplining, controlling, holding my thought in line. So my relationship to that idea is based on dependence, and if you remove my belief in it I am lost, I do not know how to think, how to evaluate. Without the belief in God, or in the idea that there is no God, I feel insecure, so I depend on that belief.

Is not our relationship with each other a state of psychological dependency? I am not talking about physiological interdependence, which is entirely different. I depend on my son because I want him to be something that I am not. He is the fulfilment of all my hopes, my desires; he is my immortality, my continuation. So my relationship with my son, with my wife, with my children, with my neighbours, is a state of psychological dependency, and I am fearful of being in a state in which there is no dependence. I do not know what that means, therefore I depend on books, on relationship, on society; I depend on property to give me security, position, prestige. And if I do not depend on any of these things, then I depend on the experiences I have had, on my own thoughts, on the greatness of my own pursuits.

Psychologically, then, our relationships are based on dependence, and that is why there is fear. The problem is not how not to depend, but just to see the fact that we do depend. Where there is attachment there is no love. Because you do not know how to love, you depend, and so there is fear. What is important is to see that fact, and not ask how to love, or how to be free from fear. You may momentarily forget your fear through various amusements, through listening to the radio, through reading the scriptures or going to a temple or church, but they are all escapes. There is not much difference between a man who takes to drink and a man who takes to religious books, between those who go to the supposed house of God and those who go to the cinema, because they are all escaping. But as you are listening, if you can really see the fact that where there is dependency in relationship there must be fear, there must be sorrow, that where there is attachment there can be no love, if as you are listening now you can just see that simple fact and comprehend it instantaneously, then you will find that an extraordinary thing takes place. Without refuting, accepting, or giving opinions about it, without quoting this or that, just listen to the fact that where there is attachment there is no love, and where there is dependency there is fear. I am talking of psychological dependency, not of your dependence on the milkman to bring you milk, or your dependence on the railway, or on a bridge. It is this inward psychological dependency on ideas, on people, on property, that breeds fear. So, you cannot be free from fear as long as you do not understand relationship, and relationship can be understood only when the mind watches all its relationships, which is the beginning of self-knowledge.

Now can you listen to all this easily, without effort? Effort exists only when you are trying to get something, when you are trying to be something. But if without trying to be free from fear, you are able to listen to the fact that attachment destroys love, then that very fact will immediately free the mind from fear. There can be no freedom from fear as long as there is no understanding of relationship, which means, really, as long as there is no self-knowledge.

The self is revealed only in relationship. In observing the way I talk to my neighbour, the way I regard property, the way I cling to belief, or to experience, or to knowledge, that is, in discovering my own dependency, I begin to awaken to the whole process of self-knowledge.

So how to overcome fear is not important. You can take a drink and forget it. You can go to the church or temple and lose yourself in prostration, in muttering words, or in devotion, but fear waits around the corner when you come out. There is the cessation of fear only when you understand your relationship to all things, and that understanding does not come into being if there is no self-knowledge. Self-knowledge is not something far away; it begins here, now, in observing how you treat others, your wife, your children. Relationship is the mirror in which you see yourself as you are. If you are capable of looking at yourself as you are without any evaluation, then there is the cessation of fear, and out of that comes an extraordinary sense of love. Love is something that cannot be cultivated; love is not a thing to be bought by the mind. If you say, "I am going to practise being compassionate," then compassion is a thing of the mind, and therefore not love. Love comes into being darkly, unknowingly, fully, when we understand this whole process of relationship. Then the mind is quiet, it does not fill the heart with the things of the mind, and therefore that which is love can come into being.

Colombo, 13 January 1957

IF YOU ARE at all serious in your intent, you have to understand the relationship between yourself and the speaker. It is not a question of someone teaching you; on the contrary, you and I as individuals are going to learn, and there is no division between the teacher and the taught. Such a division is unethical, unspiritual, irreligious. Please understand this very clearly. I am not dogmatic or assertive. As long as we do not understand the relationship between you and the speaker, we will remain in a false position. To me there is only learning, not the person who knows and the person who does not know. The moment anyone says he knows, he does not know. Truth is not to be known. What is known is a thing of the past; it is already dead. Truth is living, not static; therefore you cannot know truth. Truth is in constant movement, it has no abode, and a mind that is tethered to a belief, to knowledge, to a particular conditioning, is incapable of understanding what truth is.

SELF-KNOWLEDGE IS THE beginning of wisdom. This self-knowledge is not to be gathered from books, but you can find it for yourself through observing your daily relationship with your wife or husband, with your children, with your boss, with the bus conductor. It is through awareness of yourself in your relationship with another that you discover the workings of your own mind, and this understanding of yourself is the beginning of freedom from conditioning. If you go into it deeply, you will find that the mind becomes very quiet, really still. This stillness is not the stillness of a mind that is disciplined, held, controlled, but the stillness that comes when, through the understanding of relationship, the mind has ceased to be a centre of self-interest. Such a mind is capable of following that which is beyond the measure of the mind.

London, 18 May 1961

I THINK MOST of us know what it is to be lonely. We know that state when all relationship has been cut off, when there is no sense of the future or of the past, a complete sense of isolation. You may be with a great many people, in a crowded bus, or just sitting next to your friend, your husband or wife, and suddenly this wave comes upon you, this sense of an appalling void, an emptiness, an abyss. And the instinctive reaction is to turn away from it. So you turn on the radio, chatter, or join some society, or preach about God, truth, love, and all the rest of it. You may escape through God, or through the cinema; all escapes are the same. And the reaction is fear of this sense of complete isolation, and escape. You know all the escapes through nationalism, your country, your children, your name, your property, for all of which you are willing to fight, to struggle, to die.

Now if one realizes that all escapes are the same, and if one really sees the significance of one escape, then can you still escape? Or is there no escape? And if you are not escaping, is there still conflict? Do you follow? It is the escape from "what is," the endeavour to reach something other than "what is," that creates conflict. So a mind that would go beyond this sense of loneliness, this sudden cessation of all memory of all relationship, in which is involved jealousy, envy, acquisitiveness, trying to be virtuous and all that—must first face it, go through it, so that fear in every form withers away. So can the mind see the futility of all escapes through one escape? Then there is no conflict, is there? Because there is no observer of the loneliness; there is the experiencing of it. You follow? This loneliness is the cessation of all relationship; ideas no longer matter; thought has lost its significance. I am describing it, but please do not just listen because then afterwards you will be left with ashes. After all, the purpose of these discussions is to free oneself actually from all these terrible entanglements, to have something else in life than conflict, the fear and the weariness and boredom of existence.

Where there is no fear there is beauty, not the beauty the poets talk about and the artist paints, and so on, but something quite different. And to discover beauty one has to go through this complete isolation; or rather, you do not have to go through it, it is there. You have escaped from it, but it is there, always following you. It is there, in your heart and your mind, in the very depths and recesses of your being. You have covered it up, escaped, run away; but it is there. And the mind must experience it like a purgation by fire. Now can the mind do this without a reaction, without saying it is a horrible state? The moment you have a reaction, there is a conflict. If you accept it, you still have the burden of it, and if you deny it, you will still come across it around the corner. Without any reaction the mind *is* that loneliness; it does not have to go through it, it *is* that. The moment you think in terms of going through and reaching something else, you are again in conflict. The moment you say, "How am I to go through it, how am I really to look at it?" you are caught in conflict again.

So there is emptiness, there is this extraordinary loneliness which no Master, no guru, no idea, no activity can take away. You have fiddled with all of them, played with all of them, but they cannot fill this emptiness; it is a bottomless pit. But it is not a bottomless pit the moment you are experiencing it. Do you understand?

You see, if the mind is to be entirely free of conflict, totally, completely without apprehension, fear, and anxiety, there must be the experiencing of this extraordinary sense of having no relationship with anything. From that comes a sense of aloneness.

Don't please *imagine* that you have it; it is quite an arduous thing. It is only then, in that sense of aloneness in which there is no fear, that there is a movement towards the immeasurable, because then there is no illusion, no maker of illusion, no power to create illusion. So long as there is conflict, there is the power to create illusion, and with the total cessation of conflict all fear has ceased, and therefore there is no further seeking.

I wonder if you understand. After all, you are all here because you are seeking. And if you examine it, what are you seeking? You are seeking something beyond all this conflict, misery, suffering, agony, anxiety. You are seeking a way out. But if one understands what we have been talking about, then all seeking ceases, which is an extraordinary state of mind.

You know, life is a process of challenge and response, is it not? There is the outward challenge—the challenge of war, of death, of dozens of different things—and we respond. And the challenge is ever new, but all our responses are always old, conditioned. I do not know if this is clear. In order to respond to the challenge I must recognize it, must I not? And if I recognize it, it is in terms of the past, so it is the old, obviously. Do please see this because I want to move a little further.

To a man who is very inward, the outward challenges no longer matter, but he still has his own inward challenges and responses. Whereas I am talking of a mind that is no longer seeking, and therefore is no longer having a challenge and a response. This is not a satisfied, contented state, a cow-like state. When you have understood the significance of the outward challenge and the response, and the significance of the inward challenge that one gives to oneself and its response, and have gone through all this swiftly, not taking months and years over it, then the mind is no longer shaped by environment; it is no longer influenceable. The mind that has gone through this extraordinary revolution can meet every problem without the problem leaving any mark, any roots. Then all sense of fear has gone.

I do not know how far you have followed all this. You see, listening is not merely hearing; listening is an art. All this is a part of self-knowing; and if one has really listened and gone into oneself profoundly, it is a purification. And what is purified receives a benediction that is not the benediction of the churches.

Madras, 9 January 1966

OUR LIFE AS it is, our everyday life, is a matter of relationship. Living is a relationship. To be related implies contact, not only physically but psychologically, emotionally, intellectually. And there can be relationship only when there is great affection. I am not related to you, and you are not related to me, if what is between us is merely intellectual, verbal; that is not a relationship. There is relationship only when there is a sense of contact, a sense of communication, a sense of communion. All that implies a great affection.

As it actually is, our relationship is very confused, unhappy, contradictory, and isolated, each one trying to establish for oneself, around oneself, in oneself, an enclosure that is unapproachable. Examine yourself, not what you should be, but what you are. How unapproachable you are, each one of you, because you have so many barriers, ideas, temperaments, experiences, miseries, concerns, preoccupations. Your daily activity is always isolating you; though you may be married and have children, you are still functioning, acting, with self-centred movement. So actually there is hardly any relationship between a father and a mother, a daughter and her husband, and so on, within the community.

Unless we establish right relationship, all our lives will be constant battle, individually as well as collectively. You may say that you, as a social worker or as a Socialist, work for the community, forgetting yourself, but actually you don't forget yourself. You cannot forget yourself by identifying yourself with the greater, which is the community. That is not an act of dissipation of the "me," of the self. On the contrary it is the identification of the "me" with the greater, and therefore the battle goes on, as is so obvious in those countries where they talk a great deal about the community, about the collective. The Communist is everlastingly talking about the collective, but he has identified himself with the collective. The collective then becomes the "me" for which he is willing to struggle and go through all kinds of torture and discipline, because he has identified himself with the collective, as the religious person identifies himself with an idea that he calls God. And that identification is still the "me."

So life, as one observes, is relationship, and is based on the action of that relationship, isn't it? I am related to you, wife, husband, as a part of society. My relationship with you or with my boss brings out an action that is not only profitable to me first, but also to the community, and the motive of my identification with the community is profitable to me too. Please follow this; one has to understand the motive of one's action.

Life as it is, actually every day, is a constant battle. It is constant misery, confusion, with occasional flashes of joy, occasional expressions of deep pleasure. So unless there is a fundamental revolution in our relationship, the battle will go on, and there is no solution along that way. Please do realize this. There is no way out through this battle of relationship; yet that is what we are trying to do. We don't say, "Relationship must alter, the basis of our relationship must change." But being in conflict we try to escape from it through various systems of philosophy, through drinking, through sex, through every form of intellectual and emotional entertainment. So unless there is a radical revolution inwardly with regard to our relationship—relationship being our lives, relationship as it is now: "my wife," "my community," "my boss," "my relationship"—unless there is a radical mutation in relationship, do what you will, have the most noble ideas, talk, discuss infinitely about God and all the rest of it, it has no meaning whatsoever, because all that is an escape.

The problem arises then: How am I, living in relationship, to bring about a radical change in my relationship? I cannot escape from relationship. I may mesmerize myself; I may withdraw into a monastery, run away and become a monk, this and that, but I still exist as a human being in relationship. To live is to be related. So I have got to understand it and I have got to change it. I have to find out how to bring about a radical change in my relationship, because, after all, that produces wars; that is what is happening in this country between the Pakistanis and the Hindus, between the Muslim and the Hindu, between the Arab and the Jew. So there is no way out through the temple, through the mosque, through Christian churches, through discussing Vedanta, this, that, and the other different systems. There is no way out unless you, as a human being, radically change your relationship.

Now the problem arises: How am I to change, not abstractly, the relationship that is now based on self-centred pursuits and pleasures? That is the real question. Right?

This means really understanding desire and pleasure; *understanding*, not saying, "I must suppress desire, I must get rid of pleasure," which you have done for centuries—"You must work without desire"—I do not know what it means—"You must be desireless"—it has no meaning, because we are full of desire, burning with it. It is no good suppressing desire; it is there still, bottled up, and you put a cork on it, you discipline yourself against desire. What happens? You become hard, ruthless!

So one has to understand desire and understand pleasure, because our inward values and judgments are based on pleasure, not on any great, tremendous principles, but just on pleasure. You want God, because it gives you greater pleasure to escape from this monotonous, ugly, stupid life, which is without much meaning. So the active principle of our life is pleasure. You cannot discard pleasure. To look at that sunset, to see the leaves against that light, to see the beauty of it, the delicacy of it is a tremendous sense of enjoyment, there is a great beauty in it. Because we have denied, suppressed pleasure, we have lost all sense of beauty. In our life there is no beauty; actually there is no beauty, not even good taste. Good taste can be learned, but you cannot learn beauty. To understand beauty, you must understand pleasure.

So we have to understand pleasure, what it means, how it arises, the nature of it, the structure of it, not *deny* it. Don't let us fool ourselves and say, "My values are godly values. I have noble ideals." When you examine deep down into yourself, you will see your values, your ideas, your outlook, your way of acting, are all based on pleasure. So we are going to examine it. Not merely verbally or intellectually, we are going actually to find out how to deal with pleasure, its right place, its wrong place, whether it is worth it or not worth it. This needs very close examination.

To understand pleasure we must go into desire. We must find out what desire is, how it comes, what gives it a duration and whether desire can ever end. We have to understand how it comes into being, how it has its continuity, and whether it can ever come to an end—as it should. Unless we really understand this, this pretending to be without desire, struggling to be without desire, has no meaning; it destroys your mind, twists your mind, warps your being. And to understand whatever there is to understand, you need a very healthy, sane, clear mind, not a distorted mind, not a mind that is twisted, controlled, shaped, beaten out of its clarity.

So we are going to find out how desire comes into being. Please follow all this, because we are going to go into something else. You have to begin from the beginning to understand where this examination is going to lead us. If you are not capable of examining this, you will not be capable of understanding or examining that. So don't say, "I will skip this."

You know, it is really quite simple to understand how desire comes into being. I see that beautiful sunset. There is the seeing, and seeing the beauty of it, the colour of it, the delicacy of the leaves against the sky, the dark limb, it awakens in me the desire to keep on looking. That is: perception, sensation, contact, and desire.

Right? It is nothing very complicated. I see a beautiful car, nicely polished, with clean lines—perception. I touch it—sensation. And then desire. I see a beautiful face, and the whole machinery of desire, lust, passion, comes out. That is simple.

The next question, which is a little more complex, is: What gives desire duration, continuity? If I can understand that, then I will know how to deal with desire. You are following? The trouble begins when desire has a continuity. Then I fight to fulfil it, then I want more of it. If I can find out the time element of desire, then I know how to deal with it. We are going to go into it. I will show it to you.

We see how desire arises: seeing the car, the sunset, a beautiful face, a lovely ideal, the perfect man. (The word denies the man.) We see how desire comes into being. We are going to examine what gives desire the power, the strength, to make it last. What makes it last? It is, obviously, thought. I see the car; I have a great desire and I say, "I must have it." Thought, by thinking about it, gives it duration. The duration comes because of the pleasure I derive from the thought of that desire. Right? I see a beautiful house, architecturally and functionally excellent, and there is desire. Then thought comes in and says, "I wish I had it." Then I struggle. The whole problem begins. I cannot have it because I am a poor man; therefore it gives me frustration, and I hate; and so the whole thing begins. So the moment thought as pleasure interferes with desire, the problem arises. The moment thought, which is based on pleasure, interferes with desire, then the problem of conflict, frustration, battle begins.

So if the mind can understand the whole structure of desire and the structure of thought, then it will know how to deal with desire. That is, as long as thought does not interfere with desire, desire comes to an end. You understand? Look! I see a beautiful house and I can say that it is lovely. What is wrong with it? The house has nice proportions and is clean. But the moment thought says, "How good to have that and live in that," the whole problem begins. So desire is not wrong; desire is never wrong, but thought interfering with it creates the problem. So instead of understanding desire and understanding thought, we try to suppress desire, control desire, or discipline desire. Right?

I hope you are following all this, not merely listening, but working as hard as the speaker. Otherwise you are not partaking. You are merely listening with one ear and it is going out of the other; that is what we all do. Listening is to be attentive. And if you listen to this really, with all your heart, you will see this, and you will know then what life is, a totally different way of living.

So we are examining the machinery of thinking. The machinery of thinking is essentially based on pleasure; it is like and dislike. And in pleasure there is always pain. Obviously! I don't want pain, but I would like to have the constant continuation of pleasure. I want to discard pain. But to discard pain, I must also discard pleasure; the two cannot be divorced, they are one. So by understanding thinking, I am going to find out if the pleasure principle can be broken. You understand?

Our thinking is based on pleasure. Though we have had a great deal of pain, not only physically but inwardly, a great deal of sorrow, a great deal of anxiety, fear, terror, despair, they are all the outcome of this demand to live and establish all values in pleasure. It does not mean that you must live without pleasure, or that you must indulge in pleasure. But in understanding this whole structure of the mind and the brain, which is based deeply on pleasure, we will know how to look at desire and not interfere with it, and therefore how to end the confusion and the sorrow that may be produced by prolonging it. Right?

Thought is mechanical. It is a very good computer. It has learned a great deal, had many, many experiences, not only individual, collective, but human. It is there in the conscious as well as in the unconscious. The total consciousness is the residue, is the machinery, of all thinking. And that thinking is based not only on imitation and conformity, but always on pleasure. I conform because it gives me pleasure; I follow somebody because it gives me pleasure; I say, "He is wrong," because it gives me pleasure. When I say, "It is my country, I am willing to die for this country," it is because it gives me pleasure, which again is based on my greater pleasure of security and so on.

So thought is mechanical. It doesn't matter whose thought it is, including all your gurus, all your teachers, all your philosophers. It is the response of accumulated memory; and that memory, if you go much deeper into it, is based on this principle of pleasure. You believe in Atman, the soul, or whatever you believe in; if you go down deeply, you will see it is pleasure! Because life is so uncertain, there is death, there is fear, you hope there is something much deeper than all this, and to that you give a name; this gives you immense comfort, and that comfort is pleasure. So thought, the machinery of thinking, however complex, however subtle, however original you may think it to be, is based on this principle.

So you have to understand this, and you can only understand when you are totally attentive. Now when you listen with complete attention to what is being said, you will immediately see the truth of it or the falseness of it. There is nothing false about it, because it is factual. We are dealing with facts, not with ideas that we can discuss or about which you have your opinion or somebody's opinion. These are facts, however ugly or however beautiful. For centuries upon centuries we have thought, we have said to ourselves, "Thought can alter everything." Thought is based on pleasure, and will is the result of pleasure, and we say, "From that we will alter everything." When you examine, you will find that you cannot alter a thing, unless you understand this pleasure principle.

When you understand all this, conflict ceases. You don't end conflict deliberately, conflict ceases, which does not mean you become a vegetable. You have to understand desire, to observe it functioning daily and to watch the interference of thought, which gives desire a time element. In the examination and the understanding of this there is inherent discipline. Look! To listen to what is being said needs discipline; to listen not only verbally but inwardly, deeply, not according to some pattern. Surely the very act of listening is discipline—isn't it?

When the mind understands the nature of pleasure, thought, desire, that very examination brings with it discipline. Therefore there is no question of indulging, not indulging/should, should not; all that goes away. It is like some food you eat, which gives you a tummyache. If the pleasure of the tongue is greater than the tummyache, then you go on eating, and you constantly say, "I must not eat." You play a trick on yourself, but you go on eating. But when the pain becomes greater, then you pay attention to what you eat. But if you were attentive at the first moment when you had pain, then there would be no need to have the conflict between pleasure and pain. Are you following?

So all this brings us to a certain point, which is: that one must be completely a light to oneself. We are not, we rely on others. As you are listening, you are relying on the speaker to tell you what to do. But if you listen very carefully, the speaker is not telling you what to do. He is asking you to examine; he is telling you how to examine and what is implied in the examination. By examining very carefully, you are free of all dependence and you are a light to yourself. That means you are completely alone.

We are not alone; we are lonely. You are the result of so many centuries of culture, propaganda, influence, climate, food, dress, what people have said and have not said, and so on; therefore you are not alone. You are a result. And to be a light to yourself you have to be alone. When you have discarded the whole psychological structure of society, of pleasure, of conflict, you are alone.

And this aloneness is not something to be dreaded, something that is painful. It is only when there is isolation, when there is loneliness, that there is pain; then there is anxiety, then there is fear. Aloneness is something entirely different, because it is only the mind that is alone, that is not influenceable. This means the mind has understood the principle of pleasure and therefore nothing can touch it; nothing, no flattery, no fame, no capacity, no gift can touch it. And that aloneness is essential.

When you see the sunset attentively, you are alone—are you not? Beauty is always alone—not in the stupid, isolating sense.

It is the quality of a mind that has gone beyond propaganda, beyond personal like and dislike, that is not functioning on pleasure. A mind can perceive beauty only in aloneness. The mind has to come to that extraordinary state when it is not influenceable and therefore has freed itself from the environmental conditioning and the conditioning of tradition, and so on. It is only such a mind that can proceed in its aloneness to examine or to observe what silence is. Because it is only in silence that you can hear those screeching owls. If you are chattering with your problems and so on, you will never hear those owls. Because of silence, you hear. Because of silence, you act. And action is life.

When you understand desire, pleasure, thought, you have discarded all authority, because authority of every kind, inward, outward, has led you nowhere. You have lost all faith in all authority, inwardly; therefore you don't rely on anybody. Therefore through your examination of thought and of pleasure, you are alone. And being alone implies silence; you cannot be alone if you are not silent. And out of that silence is action. This needs further examination.

To us action is based on an idea, as a principle, a belief, a dogma, and according to that idea I act. If I can approximate that action according to my idea, I think I am a very sincere man, a very noble man. But there is always a difference between idea and action, and hence there is conflict. When there is conflict of any kind, there is no clarity. You may be outwardly very saintly, lead a so-called very simple life, which means a loin-cloth and one meal. That is not a simple life. A simple life is much more demanding and far deeper than that. A simple life is a life in which there is no conflict.

So silence comes because there is aloneness, and that silence is beyond consciousness. Consciousness is pleasure, thought, and the machinery of all that, conscious or unconscious. In that field there can never be silence; and therefore in that field any action will always bring confusion, will always bring sorrow, will always create misery.

It is only when there is action out of this silence that sorrow ends. Unless the mind is completely free from sorrow, personal or otherwise, it lives in darkness, in fear and in anxiety. Therefore, whatever its action, there will always be confusion, and whatever its choice, it will always bring conflict. So when one understands all that, there is silence, and where there is silence, there is action. Silence itself is action; not silence and then action. Probably this has never happened to you, to be completely silent. If you are silent, you can speak out of that silence, though you have your memories, experiences, knowledge. If you had no knowledge, you would not be able to speak at all. But when there is silence, out of that silence, there is action, and that action is never complicated, never confused, never contradictory.

When one has understood this principle of pleasure, thought, aloneness, and this emptiness of silence, when one has gone that far—not in terms of time, but actually—then because there is total attention, there is an act of silence in which there is total inaction, and this inaction is action. Because it is totally inactive, there is an explosion. It is only when there is a total explosion that there is something new taking place—new, which is not based on recognition and which is therefore not experienceable. Therefore it is not "I experience, and you come and learn from me how to experience."

So all these things come naturally, easily, when we understand this phenomenon of existence, which is relationship. Relationship is, with most of us, confusion, misery; and to bring about a tremendous, deep mutation, a radical change in it, one must understand desire, pleasure, thought, and also the nature of aloneness. Then out of that comes silence. And that silence, because it is totally inactive, acts when it is demanded to act; but as it is completely inactive and therefore without having any movement, there is an explosion. You know, scientists are saying that galaxies are formed when matter ceases to move and there is an explosion. It is only when there is an explosion that a new mind, a truly religious mind, comes into being. And it is only the religious mind that can solve human problems.

Rishi Valley, 8 November 1967

WHAT IS LOVE? Can we understand it verbally and intellectually, or is it something that cannot be put into words? What is it that each one of us calls love? Is love sentiment? Is love emotion? Can love be divided as divine and human? Is there love when there is jealousy or hatred, or competitive drive? Is there love when each one of us is seeking his own security, both psychological as well as worldly, outwardly? Don't agree or disagree, because you are caught in this. We are not talking of some love that is abstract; an abstract idea of love has no value at all. You and I can have a lot of theories about it, but actually, what is the thing that we call love?

There is pleasure, sexual pleasure, in which there is jealousy, the possessive factor, the dominating factor, the desire to possess, to hold, to control, to interfere with what another thinks. Knowing all the complexity of this, we say that there must be love that is divine, that is beautiful, untouched, uncorrupted; we meditate about it and get into a devotional, sentimental, emotional attitude, and are lost. Because we can't fathom this human thing called love we run away into abstractions that have absolutely no validity at all. Right? So what is love? Is it pleasure and desire? Is it love of the one and not of the many?

To understand this question—what is love?—one must go into the problem of pleasure, sexual pleasure, or the pleasure of dominating another, of controlling or suppressing another; and whether love is of the one, denying the love of the other. If one says, "I love you," does it exclude the other? Is love personal or impersonal? We think that if one loves one person, one can't love the whole, and if one loves mankind then one can't possibly love the particular. This all indicates, does it not, that we have ideas about what love should be? This is again the pattern, the code developed by the culture in which we live, or the pattern that one has cultivated for oneself. So for us ideas about love matter much more than the fact; we have ideas of what love is, what it should be, what it is not. The religious saints, unfortunately for mankind, have established that to love a woman is something totally wrong; you cannot possibly come near their idea of God if you love someone. That is, sex is taboo; it is pushed aside by the saints, but they are eaten up with it, generally. So to go into this question of what love is, one must first put away all ideas, all ideologies of what it is, or should be, or should not be, and the division as the divine and the not divine. Can we do that?

NOW CAN WE, not as a reaction but because we understand this whole process of division between the idea and the fact, put away the idea and actually face the fact, the actuality? Otherwise this division between what should be and what is, is the most deceptive way of dealing with life. The Gita, the Bible, Jesus, Krishna, all these people, these books, say, "You should, should, should." Put away all that completely; it is all ideas, ideology; then we can look at the actuality. Then one can see that neither emotion nor sentiment has any place at all where love is concerned. Sentimentality and emotion are merely reactions of like or dislike. I like you and I get terribly enthusiastic about you. I like this place, which implies that I don't like the other, and so on. Thus sentiment and emotion breed cruelty. Have you ever looked at it? Identification with the rag called the national flag is an emotional and sentimental factor, and for that factor you are willing to kill another. That is called love of your country, love of your neighbour. One can see that where sentiment and emotion come in, love is not. It is emotion and sentiment that breed the cruelty of like and dislike. And one can see also that where there is jealousy, there is no love. Obviously! I am envious of you because you have a better position, better job, better house; you look nicer, you're more intelligent, more awake, and I am jealous of you. I don't in fact say I am jealous of you, but I compete with you, which is a form of jealousy, envy. So envy and jealousy are not love and I wipe them out. I don't go on talking about how to wipe them out and in the meantime continue to be envious. I actually wipe them out as the rain washes the dust of many days off a leaf, I just wash them away.

Is love pleasure and desire, sex? Just look at what is involved in it. Is love pleasure? You know that word *love* is so loaded: "I love my country, I love that book, I love that valley, I love my king, I love my wife, I love God." It is so heavily loaded. Can we free that word, for we must use that word, from all these encrustations of centuries? We can do that only when we go into the question: Is love pleasure and desire? Conduct, we said, is based on the principle of pleasure; even when we make a sacrifice, it is still based on pleasure. You observe it throughout life. We behave in a certain way because it pleases us, essentially. And we say, if we have not thought about it a great deal, that love is pleasure. So we are going to find out whether love is beyond pleasure and if it therefore includes pleasure.

What is pleasure? From where I am sitting, through a division in the trees, I can see a hill and a rock on top of it. It is somewhat like the Italian countryside with a castle and a village on the hill. I can see the flowers with sparkling leaves in the bright sunlight. It is a great delight, it is a great pleasure. Isn't it? That scene is really most beautiful. There is the perception and the tremendous delight in it. That is pleasure, isn't it? And what is wrong with it? I look at that, and the mind says, "How lovely! I wish I could always look at that, not live in filthy towns, but live here quietly and stagnate." I want it to be repeated and tomorrow I'll come and sit here—

whether you are here or not—and look at that, because I enjoyed it yesterday and I want to enjoy it today. So there is pleasure in repetition. Right? There was the sexual enjoyment of yesterday; I want it repeated today and tomorrow. Right? I see that scene of the hill, the trees, the flowers, and there is at that moment complete enjoyment, the enjoyment of great beauty. What's wrong with it? There is nothing wrong with it, but when thought comes in and says, "By Jove, how marvellous that was, I want it repeated again," that repetition is the beginning of the desire, the looking for pleasure, for tomorrow. Then the pleasure of tomorrow becomes mechanical. Thought is always mechanical, and it builds an image of that hill, of those trees; it is the memory of it all, and the pleasure that I had must be repeated. That repetition is the continuity of desire strengthened by thought. We say, "Love is pleasure, love is desire" but is it? Is love the product of thought? The product of thought is the continuity of desire as pleasure. Thought has produced this pleasure by thinking about what was pleasurable yesterday, which I want repeated today.

So is love a continuity of thought, or has thought nothing whatsoever to do with love? One can say thought has nothing whatsoever to do with love, but one can only say that authentically when one has really understood this whole question of pleasure, desire, time, thought—which means there is freedom. Conduct can only be immediate in freedom. Look, repetitive conduct, behaviour to a pattern, breeds not only mechanical, repetitive relationship but disorder. In that there is a time element. We are asking if there is a behaviour, a conduct, which is completely free, each minute, each second; it is only in that complete behaviour, in each moment, that there is virtue, having no continuity as yesterday and tomorrow.

So freedom is in the moment of action, which is behaviour. It is not related to yesterday or tomorrow. Please look at it another way. Has love roots in yesterday and tomorrow? What has roots in yesterday is thought. Thought is the response of memory, and if love is merely memory, obviously it is not the real thing. If I love you because you were nice to me yesterday, or I don't like you because you didn't give me an opportunity for this or that, then it is a form of thought, which accepts and denies.

Can there be love that has no emotion and no sentiment, that is not of time? This is not theoretical but actual, if you really face it. Then you will find that such love is both personal and impersonal, is both the one and the many. It is like the flower that has perfume; you can smell it or you can pass it by. That flower is for everybody and, for the one who takes the trouble to breathe it deeply and look at it, a great delight.

Can we talk about this, ask questions and go into it more deeply, go into more detail, if you want to?

Questioner: When there is conflict from pressures it is impossible to bring about that state in which love is not personal. If I may also say so, in that state the word *love* disappears and we use many other words. Could we discuss that?

Krishnamurti: When there is no conflict in love, it being impersonal, would you call it by another name? Sir, again you see, we are using that word *conflict*. When does conflict arise in love? That's a dreadful question, isn't it? Do you see that? It's a dreadful statement that there is conflict in love. All our human relationships are a conflict, with the wife, the husband, with the neighbour, and so on. Why does conflict exist at all between two human beings, between husband and wife, and so on, in that relationship that we call love? Why? What does that word *relationship* mean, "to be related," what does that mean? I am related to you; that means that I can touch you, actually physically or mentally. We meet each other, there is no barrier between us, there is an immediate contact even as I can touch this microphone. But in human relationship there is no such immediate contact, because you, the husband or the wife, have an image about the wife or the husband. Don't you have an image about the speaker? Obviously. Otherwise many of you wouldn't listen. So you have a relationship with the image and if that image is not according to your pattern then you say, "He is not the right man." You actually have no contact with the speaker at all. You have a contact with the image that you have created about the speaker, just as you have an image about your wife and your husband, and the contact, the relationship between these two images is what you call relationship. The conflict is between these two images, and as long as these images exist there must be conflict. But if there is no image at all, which is something extraordinary—into which one has to go very, very deeply—if there is no image at all, there is no conflict. If you have no image about me and I have no image about you—then we meet. But if you insist that I am a foreigner and you are a dogmatic Hindu soaked in tradition, well, it becomes impossible. So where there is love there is no conflict, because love has no image. Love doesn't build images because love is not touched by thought. Love is not of time.

As you have pointed out, we are slaves to words as we are slaves to images, to symbols. The word, the symbol, is not the actuality and to find the actuality, see the actuality, one must be free of the word and the symbol.

Q: Can there be spontaneity in love?

K: Now I don't know what you mean by those words *love* and *spontaneous.* Are we ever spontaneous? Is there such a thing as being spontaneous? Have you ever been spontaneous? Have you? Ah, wait, don't agree or disagree. Look at what is implied in that word. To be spontaneous means you have never been conditioned, you are not reacting, you are not being influenced; that means you are really a free human being, without anger, hatred, without having a purpose in view. Can you be so free? Only then could you say "I am spontaneous." To be really spontaneous involves not only the understanding of the superficial consciousness, but also the deeper layers of consciousness, because all consciousness is behaviour to a pattern. Any action within the field of consciousness is limited and therefore not action that is free, spontaneous.

Claremont College, California, 17 November 1968

WE ARE DEALING not with abstractions, not with ideals, which are idiotic anyhow, but with actually "what is," which is our living. What is our living? If you observe, from the moment we are born until we die, it is a constant battle, constant struggle, with great pleasures, great fears, despair, loneliness, the utter lack of love, the boredom, the repetition, the routine. That's our life: spending forty years in an office, or in a factory, being a housewife, the drudgery, the dullness, the boredom of all that, the sexual pleasure, the jealousy, the envy, the failure of success, and the worship of success. That's our daily tortured life if you are at all serious and observe what actually is; but if you merely seek entertainment in different forms, whether it is in a church or on a football field, then such entertainment has its own pains, has its own problems. And a superficial mind does escape through the church and through the football field. We are not dealing with such superficial minds because they are really not interested. Life is serious, and in that seriousness there is great laughter. And it is only the serious mind that is living, that can solve the immense problem of existence.

I'LL EXPLAIN THIS briefly and I hope it will be clear. One is conditioned to accept envy, envy being measurement, comparison. Someone is bright, intelligent, successful, is applauded; and the other, I, am not. Through comparison, through measurement, envy is cultivated from childhood. So there is envy as an object, as something outside of oneself. Being envious, one observes it, and envy is the observer; there is no division between the observer and the observed. The observer is the envy. Please follow this a little bit. And he realizes that the observer cannot possibly do anything about envy because he is the cause *and* the effect, which is envy. So the "what is," which is our daily life, with all its problems—fear, envy, jealousy, the utter despair, the loneliness—is not different from the observer who says, "I am lonely." The observer is lonely, the observer is envy, is fear. Right? And therefore the observer cannot possibly do anything about "what is," which does not mean he accepts "what is," which does not mean he is contented with "what is." But when there is no conflict with "what is," no conflict brought about through the division between the observer and the observed, when there is no resistance to "what is," then you will find there is a complete transformation. And that is meditation—to find out for oneself the whole question of the observer, the structure and the nature of the observer, which is yourself. And the observer is the observed, which is part of you. To realize the totality of this, the unity of this, is meditation in which there is no conflict whatsoever. And therefore there is the dissolution, going beyond "what is."

From Tradition and Revolution
Rishi Valley, 28 January 1971

Krishnamurti: What does relationship mean to you?

Questioner: To be in communication.

K: What does relationship mean to you? When you look at me, at her, in what way are you related to me, to her? Are you related?

Q: I think so.

K: Let us examine it. I look at you, you look at me. What is our relationship? Is there relationship at all except a verbal relationship?

Q: There is a feeling of relationship when there is a movement towards something.

K: If both of us are moving towards an ideal, going together to a point, is that relationship? Can there be relationship when each one is in isolation?

Q: The first question you asked was, can there be relationship if there is a centre?

K: If I have built a wall around myself, consciously or unconsciously, a wall of resistance, of self-protection in order to be secure, in order not to get hurt, to be safe, is there any relationship at all? Do look at this. I am afraid, because I have been hurt physically as well as psychologically and my whole being is wounded and I do not want to be hurt any more. I build a wall around myself, of resistance, of defence, of "I know, you do not know," to feel completely safe from being further hurt. In that, what is my relationship to you? Is there any relationship?

Q: What do you mean by relationship in our daily normal life?

K: Why do you ask me? Look at yourself. In your normal, daily life, what takes place? There is the going to the office, being bullied, insulted by someone at the top. That is your relationship. With your wounded pride you come home and your wife says you are this, you are that, and you further withdraw and you sleep with her—have you any relationship?

Q: That means when the centre is there, there is no relationship at all.

Q: But there is ordinary goodwill.

K: But is there goodwill if I have got this wall of resistance, this enclosure within which I live? What is my goodwill towards you? I am polite. I keep a distance. I am always inside the wall.

Q: Even in the life of an ordinary man, there are some relationships that are not always from behind a wall.

Q: You say there is no relationship. The fact is I am related in this way because of a feeling of commitment. There is commitment to one another. I am not acting in self-interest, but only in the interest of the other.

K: You say you are acting in the interest of the other. Is that so? I follow the leader who hopes to revolutionize society, inwardly and outwardly, and I follow him and obey. I commit myself to a course of action which both the leader and I have agreed as necessary. Is there a relationship between me and the leader who is working for the same end? What does relationship mean? To be in contact with, to be in close proximity?

Q: The crux of this relationship is utility.

K: Our relationship is based on a utilitarian relationship.

Q: I see if you apply this test that there is no relationship.

K: You are not answering the deeper issue, which is, as long as there is the observer who is committing himself to a course of action, is there a relationship between you and me?

Q: Is relationship then only an idea?

K: An idea, a formula, a pattern, a goal, a principle, a utopia we both agree upon, but is there a relationship?

Q: Is there no relationship between two people?

K: It is really an enormous problem. As I said, what is relationship between one thought and another, one action and another? Or is action a continuous movement, and therefore in action there is no linking and, therefore, one action is not related to another? Look, am I related when I look at that tree? Relationship is a distance between me as the observer and the tree. The distance may be five feet two inches or a hundred yards, but where there is the distance between the observer and the observed, is there any possibility of relationship? When I am married and I have built an image of my wife and she has built an image of me, the image is the factor of distance. Is there any relationship with my wife except the physical?

We may co-operate in order to do something. To do something brings us together, but I have my own worries, she has her own agonies. We are working together, but are we related, even though we are working together for an idea?

Q: Sir, this point of working together has been understood but not the other.

K: Just a minute. To build the rocket, I believe it took three hundred thousand people, each man technologically working to create the perfect mechanism. They built a perfect rocket and each man put aside his idiosyncrasies and there was what is called co-operation. Is that co-operation? You and I work in order to build a house. We both have a common motive, but you and I are separate human beings. Is that co-operation? When I look at a tree, there is distance between me and the tree and I am not in relationship with the tree. That distance is created, not by physical space, but the distance is created by knowledge. Therefore, what is relationship, what is co-operation, what is the factor of division?

Q: Images in one form or another divide.

K: Go slowly. There is that tree. I look at it. The physical distance between me and that tree may be a few yards, but the actual distance between me and that tree is vast. Though I look at it, my eyes, mind, heart, everything is very, very far away. That distance is incalculable.
          In the same way, I look at my wife and I am very far away. In the same way I am very far away in co-operative action.

Q: Is the word, the image, interfering in all this?

K: We are going to find out. There is the word, the image, and the goal towards which both are co-operating. What is dividing is the goal. What is dividing you and me is the goal.

Q: But there is no goal with regard to the tree.

K: Just stay there. Do not jump. We think working for a goal together has brought us in contact. In fact, the goal is separating us.

Q: No. How can you say the goal is dividing us?

K: I do not know. I may be wrong. We are investigating. You and I have a goal; we work together.

Q: Is it a question of becoming?

K: Do look at it. I say goals divide people. A goal does not bring people together. Your goal and my goal are separate; they have divided us. The goal itself has divided us, not co-operation, which is irrelevant to the goal.

Q: I see one thing: where two people come together for the joy of something, that is different.

K: No. When two people come together out of affection, love, joy, then what is action that is not divisible, that does not divide? I love you, you love me, and what is action out of that love? Not a goal? What is action between two people who love?

Q: When two people come together in affection it may produce a result, but they are not coming together for the result. Therefore, in any such coming together there is no division. Whereas if two people come together with a goal, that is a divisive factor.

K: We have discovered something. Do go into it. I see that when people come together with affection, when there is no goal, no purpose, no utopia, then there is no division. Then all status disappears and there is only function. Then I will sweep the garden because it is part of the needs of the place.

Q: Love of the place.

K: No, *love.* Not love of the place. You see what we are missing. Goals divide people—a goal being a formula, a goal being an ideal. I want to see what is involved. I see what is involved. I see that as long as I have a goal, a purpose, a principle, a utopia, I see that very goal, that very principle divides people. Therefore, it is finished. Then I ask myself how I am to live, to work with you without a goal?

I see that relationship means to be in close contact so that there is no distance between the two. Right? And I see that in the relationship to the tree and myself, the flower and myself, my wife and myself, there is a physical distance and there is a vast psychological distance. Therefore, I see I am not related at all.

So what am I going to do? So I say: "Identify with the tree," "Commit yourself with the family," "Give yourself over, disown yourself in the goal and work together." All the intellectuals say, "The goal is more important than you, the whole is greater than you, so give yourself over, be completely involved with your wife, with the tree, with the world."

What am I doing? I love nature. I commit myself to the world of nature, to the family, and to an idea that we must all work together, for an end. What is happening, what am I doing in all this?

Q: Isolating myself.

K: No, sir, look at what is happening.

Q: The fact is I am not related. I struggle to build a relationship, to bridge the gap between thought and thought. I have got to build this bridge between thought and thought because unless I do this, I feel absolutely isolated. I feel lost.

K: That is only a part of it. Go into it a little more. What is happening to my mind, when my mind is struggling to commit itself to everything, to family, to nature, to beauty, to working together?

Q: There is a lot of conflict there, sir.

K: I realize, as A has pointed out, I am not related to anything. I have come to that point. Then, not being related to anything, I want to be related; therefore I commit myself, therefore I involve myself in action and yet the isolation goes on. So what is going on in my mind?

Q: Death.

Q: There is a constant struggle.

K: You see you have not moved away from that point. I am not related and then I try to be related. I try to identify myself through action. Now what is taking place in the mind? I am moving into peripheral commitment. What happens to my mind when it moves on the outside all the time?

Q: The mind gets strengthened.

Q: I am escaping from myself.

K: Which means what? Do look at it. Nature becomes very important, the family becomes very important, the action to which I have completely given myself over becomes all-important, and what has happened to me? I have completely externalized everything. Now what has happened to the mind that has externalized the whole movement of relationship? What happens to your mind when it is occupied with the external, with the periphery?

Q: It has lost all sensitivity.

K: Do look at what happens inside you. In reaction to the externalization, you withdraw, you become a monk. What happens to the mind when it withdraws?

Q: I am incapable of spontaneity.

K: You will find the answer. Look in there. What happens to your mind when you withdraw or when you are committed? What happens when you withdraw into your own conclusions? It is another world. Instead of one world, you create another world, which you call the inner world.

Q: The mind is not free.

K: Is that what is happening to your mind?

Q: It is always committed.

K: The mind is committed to the outward phenomena and the re-action to that is the inward commitment, the withdrawal. The inward commitment is the reaction of your own world of imagination, of mystical experience. What happens to the mind that is doing this?

Q: It is occupied.

K: Is that what is going on? She says it is occupied. Is that all? Put your guts into it. The mind externalizes its activity and then withdraws and acts. What happens to the quality of the mind, to the brain that is withdrawing and externalizing?

Q: It does not face the fact.

Q: There is a great fear. It becomes dull.

Q: It is not free to look.

K: Have you watched your mind when it is externalizing all action outwardly and all action inwardly? It is the same movement—the outer and inner. It is like a tide going out and coming in. It is so simple, is it not? What happens to the mind going out, coming in?

Q: It becomes mechanical.

K: It is a mind that is completely without any bearing, completely unstable, a mind that has no order. It becomes neurotic, unbalanced, disproportionate, inharmonious, destructive, because there is no stability in the whole movement.

Q: It is restless.

K: Therefore, there is no stability. Therefore what happens? It invents another outside action or withdraws. And the brain needs order, order means stability. It tries to find order out there in relationship and does not find it; so it withdraws and tries to find order within and again is caught in the same process. Is this a fact?

The mind tries to find stability in co-operative action about something. The mind tries to find stability in the family, in commitment and does not find it and so translates, seeks relationship with nature, becomes imaginative, romantic, which again breeds instability. It withdraws into a world of infinite conclusions, utopias, hopes, and again there is no stability, and therefore it invents an order in that. The mind being unstable, narrow, not rooted in anything, gets lost. Is that what is happening to you?

Q: That explains the cult of the beautiful.

K: Cult of the beautiful, cult of the ugly, cult of the hippies. Is that what is happening to your mind? Beware. Do not accept what I am saying.

A mind that is not stable, in the sense of firm, deeply rooted in order—not an invented order, for an invented order must be death—such a mind is the most destructive mind. It goes from communism to the guru, to Yoga Vashista, to Ramana Maharshi and back again. It is caught in the cult of the beautiful, the cult of the ugly, the cult of devotion, of meditation, and so on.

How is the mind to be completely still? From that stillness, action is entirely different. See the beauty of it.

Q: That is the dead end of the mind.

K: No, sir. I am asking myself, how is this mind to be completely still? Not stability in the sense of hardness, but a stability that is flexible. A mind that is completely stable, firm, deep, has its roots in infinity. How is that possible? Then what is the relationship with the tree, with the family, with the committee?

I realize my mind is unstable, and I understand what it means. I know now for myself, I have understood for myself that this movement is born of instability. I know that and so I negate that. And I ask what is stability? I know instability with all its activity, with all its destruction and when I put that away completely, what is stability? I sought stability in family, in work, and I have also inwardly sought stability in withdrawal, in experience, in knowledge, in my capacity, in God. I see I do not know what stability is. The not knowing is the stable.

The man who says "I know" and therefore "I am stable" has led us to this chaos—people who say, "We are the chosen ones." The vast number of teachers, gurus have said "I know."

Rejecting all that, rely on yourself. Have confidence in yourself. And when the mind puts away all this, when it has understood what is not stable and that it cannot know what is true stability, then there is a movement of flexibility, of harmony, because the mind does not know. The truth of not-knowing is the only factor from which one can move. The truth of that is the stable. A mind that does not know is in a state of learning. The moment I say I *have* learned, I have stopped learning and that stopping is the stability of division.

So I do not know. The truth is I do not know. That is all. And that gives you a quality of learning and in learning there is stability. Stability is in the "I *am* learning," not, "I *have* learned." See what it does to the mind. It completely unburdens the mind and that is freedom; the freedom of not-knowing. See the beauty of it—the not-knowing, therefore, freedom. Now what happens to the brain that functions in knowledge? That *is* its function, is it not? To function from memory to memory. In knowledge the mind has found tremendous security, and biologically that security is necessary. Otherwise it cannot survive. Now, what happens to the brain that says I really do not know anything except the biological knowledge of survival? What happens to the rest of the brain? The rest of the brain before was tethered. Now it is not occupied. It will act, but it is not occupied.

That brain has never been touched. It is no longer capable of being hurt. There is a new brain born or the old brain is purged of its occupations.

San Francisco, 10 March 1973

ONE HAS TO find out what it means to observe, to observe your relationship with another, however intimate or however distant. Observation implies total attention. Please do this as we are talking, not as a group therapy, which is a horror, or some kind of group entertainment, which is absurd, but observe actually "what is" so that there is no distortion, so that prejudice, tendencies, various forms of inclinations don't enter into it. Pure observation without distortion means attention. This attention comes naturally; you don't have to go to college or practise or all the rest of the absurdity that is going on when you are really deeply interested. If you are not, then there is something radically wrong. When the house is burning, when there is so much catastrophe going on, not to be interested, not to be totally concerned or totally committed to the resolution of the problem, indicates a mind that is totally dead. So, to observe your relationship and to transform it.

Transformation takes place in relationship—in which there is division and hence conflict, jealousy, anxiety, insecurity, violence, and all the rest of those things born out of division—through observation. Observe what goes on. If you observe you will see that your relationship with another is based on knowledge, knowledge which is the past, knowledge which becomes the image about another. Listening to the speaker, you have an image about the speaker, which is obvious, otherwise you wouldn't be here. Your image of the speaker is based on reputation, propaganda, books, and all the rest of it. Actually, you don't know the speaker at all, but you have an image about him. Therefore that image divides. You have an image about your wife, your girlfriend, boyfriend, that image is built on knowledge of past events, happenings. And this image, which is born out of knowledge in relationship, brings about division. That's a fact; we don't have to go into it, argue or analyse, it is so. And these images, verbal, structural, romantic, intellectual, emotional, and so on, all bring about a basic fundamental division. You have an image about yourself, that you must be this or that, and you have an image about the other, so your relationship is between these two images and therefore there is no actual relationship, and hence conflict.

Now can that structure of relationship be totally changed, radically transformed? Then we will create a totally different society. And it is only possible when we are sharing, thinking, creating together. In this there is no authority whatsoever because you are observing your own self, your own image of yourself and the image that you have created about another, which creates division.

Then the question arises: How is it possible not to create images at all? You understand? I hope we are following each other, are we? Is it possible for the mind that has been cultivated, that has acquired tremendous knowledge through experience, which is the past, this mind that has so many images, so many conclusions, that is so heavily conditioned, can this mind be free of all images? If it is not, then life becomes a constant battle. Right? Is this question clear?

Knowledge in relationship creates division. That is, when you have a relationship with your husband or a girl, or whoever it is, gradually knowledge enters into that relationship, knowledge being what you have acquired, remembered, experienced in that relationship. So knowledge becomes a barrier in relationship. Right? Are we taking a journey together?

Audience: Yes.

Krishnamurti: Good! You know this is very important because to take a journey together with somebody we must have that quality of affection that shares, that isn't merely listening to a verbal description. The description is not the described; the word is not the thing. If you are merely following it verbally then we are not journeying together; there is not the clarity in the investigation that is so essential. So you are not following the speaker. If you are following the speaker then the speaker becomes the authority, and you have got sufficient authority in the world already, don't add another. It is freedom from authority that is necessary. Authority means the authority of someone to tell you what to do. Then you depend on somebody, and in that all the problems of authority arise. Whereas if you learn how to observe, how to be completely committed to attention in relationship, you see that you cannot learn from another. This has to be learned as you go along, you cannot learn it from a book. So if I may suggest, use the speaker as a mirror in which you see yourself. And when you learn to see yourself in that mirror, then break the mirror so that you are free from the speaker, so that you observe yourself what is actually going on.

As we said, we have a great many images, conclusions, and so the mind is never free to observe. Having accumulated these conclusions through education, through relationship, through propaganda, in a thousand different ways, the mind functions with conclusions, therefore mechanically. But relationship is not mechanical, even though we have reduced relationship to a routine, to a mechanical process.

We have to understand very deeply the meaning of the word *knowledge* and the meaning of freedom from knowledge in relationship. Knowledge is necessary; you and the speaker cannot possibly communicate verbally without knowing English. To do anything functionally, technologically, knowledge is necessary—how to ride a bicycle and all the rest of it. To function efficiently, objectively, rationally, knowledge is necessary, but we use function to achieve status. And when there is the pursuit of status in function there is division and hence conflict between function and status, which is part of our relationship with each other. When you are seeking status in function, then to you status is far more important than function, and hence in that there is conflict inwardly as well as outwardly. We have to observe this, to observe how the mind works in relationship, that through function it is seeking status and therefore in relationship there is conflict, and also that there is conflict where there is division between you and another, where knowledge about your husband, your boy, girl, or whoever, acts as division. Therefore it is only when the mind is free, or rather is aware, that it sees the function of knowledge and the necessity of knowledge and sees the danger, the poison of knowledge in relationship. I hope this is clear.

Look, if I am married to you and I have lived with you, I have accumulated a great deal of knowledge about you in that relationship. That knowledge has become the image of you. You have given me pleasure, sex, insulted me, nagged me, bullied me, dominated me, saying, "Women are more important than men"—you know everything that is going on in the world. How childish all this is, how utterly immature. I have built an image about you. It may be one day old or ten years old. That image divides me from you, and you have an image about me. So our relationship is between these two images and therefore there is no relationship at all. Realizing this, is it possible to live in this world with knowledge, which is absolutely necessary, and with freedom from knowledge in relationship? Because when there is freedom from knowledge in relationship, division ceases and therefore conflict in relationship comes to an end. As it is, one observes in the world more and more conflict; misery, confusion, sorrow is everywhere. And the mind is in a state of anxiety in relationship when it is concerned only with knowledge and not with wisdom. And wisdom comes into being only when there is an understanding of knowledge and the freedom from the known.

So our question is: Can the mind, which functions with conclusions, with images, can that mind be free, not tomorrow, not within a given period of time but be out of this conflict altogether? And that is only possible when you can learn how to observe, how to observe yourself and another. It is far more important to observe yourself and not the other, because what you are, the other is; you are the world and the world is you, the two are not separate. The society that you have created is you. This society, the ugliness, the brutality, the extravagance, the pollution, all the things that are going on are the result of your daily activity, so you are society, you are the world and the world is you. This is not a mere verbal statement but an actual fact. And to observe this the mind must be free to look, free from distortion of opinions, conclusions; then the mind is fresh to look, to learn.

You know there is a difference between learning and acquiring knowledge. Most of us at college, university and so on, are very good at acquiring knowledge. To us that is learning: to accumulate facts, correlate them with other facts and data. Our minds, our brains are full of knowledge of the past. Knowledge *is* the past, and we are all the time adding to that knowledge; and it is necessary when you function as an engineer or as a scientist, when you drive a car or speak a language. But learning, it seems to me, is something entirely different. Learning is a constant movement. There is a constant movement in learning so that there is never an accumulation. For the accumulation is the "me," the "me" that separates you and hence there is conflict. Wherever there is "me" there must be conflict because it is the very core of division.

And love cannot be learned. Knowledge cannot acquire either wisdom or love. It is therefore very important to understand the whole structure of relationship because that is the basis of our life. From that all action takes place. If action is merely the continuation of knowledge then it becomes mechanical. And our relationship becomes mechanical when it is based on routine and knowledge. When there is freedom from the known then relationship changes totally.

❖

Is ONE ATTENTIVE to our relationship? That's what we have been talking about, not about flowers and the clouds. Are you deeply, non-verbally, without conclusions, aware of your relationship? Or are you afraid to face your relationship, or afraid to look, because when you do look it will bring up all kinds of things, therefore you would rather avoid it? Attention is not something specifically given to a particular problem. Attention is a state of mind that is totally committed to finding a way of living in which conflict of any kind has come to an end. Because if that conflict in human relationship ceases then we will bring about a totally different kind of culture.

Saanen, 1 August 1973

WHAT IS THE relationship between me and you, with my wife, my husband, my daughter, my son, if I have no image? What is my relationship with you if I have no image about you?... You have to find this out; you can't just answer. Look, I have lived with you, and all the troubles, the travails, the anxiety, all that has built an image in my mind. But if I have no image about you, what is my relationship then? If you are really honest you can't answer this question. You can only answer it if you really have no image at all. And that is one of the most radical things in life, not to have an image about the mountains, about another, about the person you live with, and all the rest of it, not to have a single image, about the country, anything. Image means opinion, idea, conclusion, symbol, the thought that builds up all the images. Then what is the relationship between you, who have an image, and the person who has no image? Don't answer me. This you have to find out. That is love. The other thing is not love. Right?

WE NEED MEMORY in order to ride a bicycle. I need memory in order to talk English and so convey something to you, if you are interested in what I want to communicate. I need memory to function in a factory, in a business, and so on. But that memory in relationship is the image. I have built an image about you, and you have built an image about me, therefore our relationship is between these two images. And that is what is so important to us—the image I have about you and the image you have about me, and we live with these images. This relationship is called love; in this relationship there is attachment and all the rest of it, and we cling to it, the image. And we say the mind does it because it feels secure in having something, in having an image. If it has no image it is empty, and we are afraid of being empty and therefore we say we must be something.

So can the mind observe the present, the "what is," without the memory, the image, the conclusion, the opinion, the judgment, the evaluation of the past? Just to observe "what is." Let me put it round the other way. Go much deeper, very much deeper. I love my brother, my son, my wife, my girl, my boy, and he dies. The fact is he is dead. That is "what is." Right? Can the mind observe "what is" without any movement of thought, which is the past? You understand?

Let's go on. Look, my son is dead, that is a fact. Then what takes place? The image I have built about my son through the years makes the mind feel empty, lonely, sorrowful, self-pitying, and there is the hope that I will meet my son in a next life, so I go to a medium, a seance to get in touch with him, all that business. That is, the mind doesn't observe, live completely with "what is," without the image. You understand? Come on, sirs. When I have no self-pity, I don't say, "Oh, I wish my son had lived, he would have been such a marvellous human being." Do you follow? I have no movement of thought at all. The mind lives only with the fact that my son is dead. Have you ever done this? Yes or no?

Questioner: My mind becomes quiet.

Krishnamurti: No, sir, I am not talking of quietness. Look, sir, this happens to every living human being; death is there. What takes place in you when you look at the fact without a single image? I can't tell you unless you come to it.

Q: You see what actually is.

K: Yes, sir, I said that. Living, being with what actually has taken place, not to deviate, not to run away, not let thought say this and that—nothing.

Q: It is quiet now.

K: You will find out. I hope nobody dies whom you love, or you think you love; I hope you will never suffer, but when you come to that, as inevitably everybody in the world does, not only those people living in Vietnam and Cambodia but every day it is happening around you, then you will find out what it means to live with "what is" completely, without a single image. I insult you, I say terrible things about you, can you listen to me without the movement of thought that creates an image that hurts? Can you listen? Try it. Do it, and then you will see what an extraordinary change takes place, a change in which there is complete negation of every form of image, therefore the mind is never burdened with the past. It's like having a young mind, you understand.

Saanen, 2 August 1973

THE CULTURE IN which the mind has grown, been cultivated, educated, has accepted confusion as the way of life. It says, "Yes, I am confused and let's get on with it. Don't make a lot of noise about it; let's get on with it." And one nice day I realize I am really confused, parts of me are, parts of me are not, and so on. The culture has brought me up in this, has educated this mind, educated it to live in confusion and disorder. And it has brought a great deal of sorrow, misery. And the mind says, "There must be a way out of all this." And it begins to learn to look at itself. It realizes it can only look at itself when there is no movement of thought, because thought has created this mess, this culture. So it realizes it can only observe clearly when there is no movement of thought. Is that possible? So it tests it out. It doesn't accept it, it says, "I am going to test it, find out if it is possible." So it looks at things, the mountains, the hills, the rivers, the trees and people. It can look outwardly comparatively easily, without the interference of thought. But it becomes much more difficult when it looks inwardly. The inward perception is always with the desire to do something about that which it perceives. And so one realizes it is again the activity of thought. So it regards everything, observes, and realizes as long as there is an observer this process of choice, conflict must exist. So is it possible to observe without the observer, which is the past, experience, all that, to observe without the observer? That demands great attention.

That attention brings its own order, which is discipline. There is no question of imposing an order. That very experiment, that very testing of observation without the observer brings its own order, its own sense of complete attention. And the mind observes without the observer, and remains totally unmoving, immobile with regard to "what is." Right? Then what takes place?

See what the mind has done. It has not been able to resolve "what is," so it has wasted its energy in trying to escape from it, suppress it, analyze it, explain, and so on. When it has not wasted its energy, remaining completely with "what is," the mind has all its energy. You understand? Not a spark of energy is wasted. There is no escaping, there is no naming, there is no trying to overcome it, suppress it, make it conform to a pattern, and so on. All those are a wastage of energy. Now when that energy is not wasted, the mind is full of this energy and is observing actually "what is." Then is there "what is"? Then is there confusion?

To see all that is not only the truth but the wisdom of it. And out of that wisdom comes intelligence that will operate in daily life, that will not create confusion—do you understand?—in moments of negligence it may do something, but it will correct it immediately. You follow? So that intelligence is all the time in operation. It is not my intelligence or your intelligence.

Have we taken the journey together, a little bit at least?

Questioner: In such kind of action there is no actor.

Krishnamurti: Now what is the action of that intelligence in relationship? You understand? Life is relationship—between man and woman, between nature and man or woman, between human beings. And so I am asking what the action is of that intelligence that is born out of wisdom, that comes out of the perception of truth. What is the action of that intelligence in human relationship? Because I have to live in this world. Right? I have a wife, children, family, the boss, the factory, shop and so on, so what is the action of that intelligence in my relationship with another? Come on, ask!

Q: How can you say beforehand what will happen?

K: How can you say what the action of intelligence will be before-hand? I don't know what the action of intelligence is beforehand, but we are inquiring now. What is the action of that intelligence in relationship? I am related to you. I am actually related to you because you are sitting there and I am sitting here, you are listening to me, we are sharing this together, we are observing this thing together, "cooking" it together; therefore we are related, not in the sense of being intimate, but as human beings we are related because it is our common problem, it is our human problem. So we are asking: We are related, how does this intelligence act in this relationship?

Q: It must be love. Out of that intelligence comes love.

K: I don't know. That's an idea. You see, sir, my mind will not accept a theory, an idea, a conclusion, speculation. It will only—my mind, not yours—this mind will only move from fact to fact, from "what is" to "what is," and nothing more.

Q: We must use words in this dialogue, and the moment we use words we are concerned with ideas, but the kind of dialogue you are insisting upon is almost impossible for most of us.

K: Look, there is communication through words and communication through non-words, non-verbal as well as verbal communication. If I know how to listen to you, to the words that you are using, to the meaning of the words that you are using, which is common to both of us, if I really know how to listen to you verbally, then I also know how to listen to you non-verbally, because I can pick it up.

I am asking a very simple question that will lead to a great deal of investigation, which is: What is the action of the insight that has brought about this quality of intelligence in my relationship with another human being? Until I solve this, my relationship must create misery, not only for you but for me also. So I must apply my whole being to find out. It isn't a casual, superficial investigation, because my life depends on it. I don't want to live in suffering, in confusion, in this appalling mess that civilization, culture, has put me in. Therefore my intelligence says, "Find out!" Because you cannot live alone, there is no such thing as living alone. There is only isolation, which this culture has encouraged; in the business world, in the religious world, in the economic world, in the artistic world, in every world, in every sphere, it has encouraged me to be isolated: "I am an artist," "I am a writer," "I am far superior to everybody else," "I am a scientist," or, "I am nearest to God."

So I know very well what isolation is, and to live in that isolation and have relationship with another means absolutely nothing. So my intelligence says, "That's absurd, you can't live that way." Therefore I am going to find out how to live in relationship and what the activity of that intelligence is in that relationship.

I want to know. Please test it out for yourself and ask yourself that question. You see what this intelligence is? It is the outcome of having an insight into the reality of "what is," and the observation of that is wisdom and the perception of it is truth. The daughter of truth is wisdom, and intelligence is the daughter of wisdom. I have seen that. Now I am asking myself: What is the action of that intelligence in relationship? In relationship has it any image? Is my mind building an image about you who live in the same house as I do? You may nag me, you may bully me, you may threaten me, dominate me, you may give me sexual pleasure, and so on—does the mind build images?

Q: No.

K: Don't ever say, no, sir; find out! That requires great attention, doesn't it? You can't just say yes or no. It requires complete attention to find out if you have an image and why the image comes into being. Just listen, sir. I am stopping you from saying yes or no. That's all. Let's investigate. Let's share this problem together. When you say no or yes, you have stopped it. But if I say, "Look, let's find out, let's inquire, see what is involved in this," in that, I haven't created an image about you at all. I have said, "Please stop and look at what we are doing."

Is the mind creating an image? If it is, then it is not the activity of intelligence because it sees how images divide people, as nationalities have divided people, religions have divided people, gurus have divided people, the books, the Bible, the Bhagavad Gita, the Koran, have divided people. So the image, symbols, conclusions divide people. Where there is division there must be conflict. And therefore an action born out of conflict is a non-intelligent action. So intelligent action is an action that is without friction, without conflict. When I am related to you and I have an image, it is a stupid action, an unintelligent action. So I see that. Am I creating an image about you when you call me a fool, when I depend on you for my physical pleasure, or depend on you for my money, for your support, for your companionship, for your encouragement? Dependence is an action of a mind that is not intelligent.

So I am beginning to discover, learn, what relationship is when intelligence comes into being. You are following all this? It is so astonishingly simple, really simple.

Q: It is simple but not easy.

K: What is simple is the easiest, most practical thing, not all your complicated things. They have led to impracticality, to all this mess, which is the result of utter futility. Look, what is simple is to see the truth that images divide people. That is simple, isn't it? And seeing the simplicity of it is the act of intelligence, and that intelligence will act in my relationship with you. So I am watching how that intelligence is going to operate. You understand? I am related to my wife, my mother, my sister, my girl, whatever it is. I am watching. I am watching to see how that intelligence operates. You understand? And it sees the moment you create an image you are back in the old world, you are back in a rotten civilization. And the mind is watching, learning, and therefore intelligence opens the door to a life that is completely simple.

Brockwood Park,
8 September 1973

IN WHAT WE call love there is dependence, the sense of attachment that comes from loneliness, insufficiency in oneself, not being able to stand alone, therefore leaning on somebody, depending on somebody. We depend on the milkman, the railwayman, the policeman. I am not talking of that kind of dependence, but of psychological dependence with all its problems: the problems of image in relationship, the image that the mind has built about the other, and the attachment to that image, and the denial of this image and creating another image. All that is what we call love. And the priests have invented another thing, the love of God, because it is much easier to love God, an image, an idea, a symbol created, put together by the mind or by the hand than to find out what love is in relationship.

Are you following all this? So what is love? It is part of our consciousness, this thing called love in which there is the "me" and the "you'; the "me" attached to you, possessing, dominating; you possessing me, dominating, holding. You satisfy my physical, sexual demands, and I satisfy you economically and so on. All that is what we call love. And is that love? Romantic love, physical love, the love of one's country for which you are willing to kill, maim, destroy yourself, is that what love is? Obviously love is not emotionalism, sentimentality, the sloppy acceptance of—you know—"I love you and you love me." Talking about the beauty of love, the beautiful people, is all that love?

LOOK, MAKE IT very simple. All relationship is based on the image that you have built about another and the other has built about you. Right? You can't argue about it, it is so. And these two images have relationships. These images are the result of many years of memories, experiences, knowledge, which you have built about her, and she has built about you. That is part of your consciousness. What is the relationship when there is no image at all between you and her, and she has no image about you? You understand? If I may ask, are you aware that you have an image about him to which you are dreadfully attached? Are you aware that you have an image about her to which you cling? Are you aware of this, conscious of it? If you are conscious of it, you see that your relationship with her, or hers with you, is based on those images. Can those images come to an end? Then what is relationship? If the image has come to an end, which is the content of consciousness that makes up your consciousness, when the various images you have about yourself, about everything, come to an end, then what is the relationship between you and her? Then is there an observer observing apart from the thing it has observed? Or is it a total movement of love in relationship? Are you getting it? So love is a movement in relationship in which the observer is not.

So the mind—we are using the word *mind* to include the brain, the physical organism, the totality—that mind has lived within the field of fragmentations, which make up its consciousness, and without its content the observer is not. And when the observer is not, then relationship is not within the field of time that exists when there is the image you have about her and she has about you. Can that image come to an end as you live daily? If that image doesn't come to an end then there is no love. It is then one fragment against another fragment.

Now you have heard that, don't draw a conclusion from it. See the truth of it; and you can't see the truth of it verbally. You can hear the meaning of the words but you have to see the significance of it, have an insight into it, actually see the truth of "what is." Then the truth is not within the field of consciousness.

Saanen, 25 July 1974

IS THERE SECURITY at all? Mind has sought security in things, physical things, property, in a name, in a characteristic activity, and so on. It has sought security in concepts, ideals, formulas, systems. And when one looks at all that very closely, objectively, non-sentimentally, non-personally, then you will see that whole set-up brings insecurity for everybody. And yet the mind, the brain must have security to function. So I am asking you, and myself, if there is this thing called security at all? Right? Now that is what we are going to investigate. That is what we are going to find out. But if I find out, and I tell you, then we shall not be sharing. So, together we are going to find out.

You see the truth of the necessity of physical security and yet the mind too is always pursuing security in different forms, security being something permanent, a permanent relationship, a permanent house, a permanent idea. Now is there such a thing as permanency? I may want it because I see everything around me fading away, withering, in a flux, but the mind says, there must be security, permanency. But there is no permanency in an idea, in a concept, no permanency in things, for various reasons, or without my understanding why. And then I seek permanency in my relationships, in my wife, in my children, and so on. Is there a permanent security in relationship? You understand? Ask yourself! When you want permanency in relationship the whole problem of attachment arises. Please do it; for your own sake, do watch it. And when you are attached, the whole problem of fear, loss, suspicion, hate, jealousy, anxiety, all that enters into that problem, into that desire to have permanent relationship. You understand? One has found there is no permanency in a concept, though the Catholics, the Protestants, the Communists have indoctrinated the mind, and the mind has accepted such doctrine as permanent. But you can see it is disappearing, it is fading away, they are questioning everything. And also one sees there is no permanency in any physical thing. So the mind says, "I must have personal relationship." And then we see the implications of that relationship, a relationship based on an image of you and of the other, each one having an image about the other, which is impermanent, and yet seeking permanency in that relationship.

So one asks: Is there anything permanent? It is a very difficult question to ask, if you are at all serious, and a very difficult thing to find out what happens to a mind that has found the truth that there is nothing permanent. Will it go off, become insane? Will it take a drug, commit suicide? Will it again fall into the trap of another ideology, another desire that will project a permanent thing? You follow?

❖

ONE HAS DISCOVERED by looking, not analyzing, by just observing our daily, everyday life, that the mind has sought security in all these things. And thought says, "There is no security, there is nothing permanent." And it begins to seek something more permanent. It has not found anything permanent here, therefore it is seeking a permanency in another area, in another consciousness. But thought itself is impermanent—right?—but it has never asked if it is itself impermanent. You understand what I am saying?

Please, this demands tremendous care; don't go off the deep end. So when the mind says there is nothing permanent, it includes thought. Look at it! Can the mind be sane, healthy, whole, and therefore act totally, when it realizes there is nothing permanent? Or will it become insane? You follow? When you are confronted with this problem that there is nothing permanent, including the structure of thought, can you stand it? You understand? Can you see the significance of saying there is *nothing* permanent, including yourself, including all the structure that thought has built, and that it says is "me"? That "me" is also impermanent. I wonder if you see all this? Leave it there for the moment, we'll come to it in a different way.

We have also to understand this question of time. Time means movement—right?—from here to there, physically. To cover the distance from here to there you need time, time by the watch, time by the sun, time by day or time by year. What is the relationship of time, which is distance, movement, to thought? Please, this is not difficult; just listen to it and you will see it for yourself. The whole Western world is principally, essentially based on measurement, technologically, spiritually—the hierarchy, the top dog, the top bishop, the top archbishop, the pope; it is all based on measurement socially, morally, and obviously technologically. And the saint also is the supreme measure, accepted by the church or by the religion. So the whole moral, intellectual structure of our civilization is based on that—time, measurement, thought. Right? Thought is measurement, thought is time, time being yesterday. What I did yesterday modifies the present and this modification continues in a different form in the future. The movement from the past through the present to the future is time, which is measurable.

And there must be time to go from here to there. I need time to learn a language or any technique. But does the mind need time to transform itself? You are following all this? The moment the mind admits time in order to transform itself, it is still within the field of measurement, time, thought. That area has been created by thought, and to change itself, to bring about a different mind, if it still functions within that same field, then there is no change at all. May I go on? I hope you are following all this.

I'll put it this way. I am greedy and I know greed is comparative. I have this feeling of greed that arises when I see something more than I have, which is a measure, right? And I ask myself:

To transform that feeling, that measurement, is time necessary? If time becomes a necessity, then I still remain within the field of measure. Therefore I have not changed greed at all. You have seen this? So is there a change that is not based on cause, which is time, but change that is instantaneous? Please, *you* are asking all these questions, not I only.

I am violent. Unfortunately, for various reasons, human beings are violent beings, we all know that. To change violence, to transform it so that the mind is never violent, does it take time? If you admit time is needed, then that violence takes another form because it is still within the same area. Have some of you got it? If you have, tell others.

So I am asking, is the desire for permanency the cause of the action of permanency that is still within the field of time? Does the cause, the motive, make me desire permanency, and so on? So cause brings about the structure of time. Now I ask: Is there any permanency at all?

Now let's look at it. We have looked at time, permanency, and now we are going to look at our daily life, which is based on that. Right? There is desire for permanency in relationship because that is becoming more and more real, because we have discarded all the others, the intellectual permanencies of theories, state-worship, church, and so on. We have discarded those, and so we say there must be permanent relationship. That is the only thing we have, and in that too we find there is nothing permanent. Can the mind, your mind, face this absolute truth that there is no permanency, see this, not just theorize about it?

Then let us look at the immense problem that man has never been able to solve: this question of death. They are all related.

❖

YOU SEE, THE ancient Hindus, who were very clever people, thought, "This is impossible; man can't let go of everything instantly." Therefore the idea of "me," as you hold to it, must go on, the "me" which is the result of time, measurement, thought, of course. Right? That "me" must evolve slowly through various lives, until it reaches the highest excellence, which is Brahman, God, whatever you like to call it. So they had that idea. The Christians have it in a different way, not so mathematically, not so cleverly worked out, without such subtle implications involved in it. I will not go into all that. What is implied is that the next life becomes very important, therefore this life is important. This life becomes tremendously important because, depending on how you behave now, if you behave rightly, you will be rewarded next life. You understand? That is the belief. They all believe in it, but still nobody behaves *now*.

So they carry on this game.

So can the mind see this whole tremendous phenomenon? I cannot go into all the details of it. It is such a vast area in which the mind has sought security. Mind has created time, as thought, as measurement. And in that measurement, in that time, it has a movement in which it has tried to find permanency, as the "me" and "you," and so on. We are asking: Seeing all of this enormous, very complex and extraordinarily subtle area, can the mind see the truth that there is absolutely no permanency? Which is really death. You understand?

Can you see the truth of this? Not accept the truth of another; then it is not truth, it is mere propaganda, which is a lie. Can you, for yourself, after all this explanation, see the truth of it? Not verbal truth, not the intellectual concept, saying, "Yes, I have understood it." That is not truth. *Truth* means it *acts*. It acts, and so you see that there is no permanency. Then you are no longer attached. You are no longer attached to an idea, a concept, a religious belief, a dogma, a saviour. So now what takes place. You follow? When you see the truth of that, there is freedom, and freedom means total intelligence—I wonder if you see this—not the intelligence of cunning thought but that supreme intelligence that has seen the truth and therefore is free of the things that thought has created. And that quality of intelligence, which is supreme and excellent in its essence, can operate. You follow? Therefore there is security in *that*, not in this. I wonder if you are getting all this? Then you can live in this world, with things or with nothing; you understand? So *that* is immortal. You understand? That intelligence which is neither yours nor mine, which does not belong to any church, to any group, that is the highest form of intelligence and therefore in that there is complete and total security. Mind cannot create that intelligence. It takes place when you see the truth of the obvious, when you see the false as the false. Then the mind is no longer caught in the network of thought, and that intelligence can then operate in our daily life and there is permanency. Right? Got it?

Dialogue with Students and Staff: Brockwood Park, 30 May 1976

Krishnamurti: We are trying to find out what is right action in relationship. We took an example of hurt. If that hurt continues through the present, modified to the future, that movement of hurt cannot bring about right action. That's clear. Who is hurt? We said the hurt comes when there is the image. That image is the "me," the "me" is not different from the image. Before, we separated the "me" from the image, and then the "me" said, "I will make an effort to get rid of that hurt." Right? "I'll battle with it, I'll suppress it, I'll go to an analyst, I'll do anything to get rid of that hurt." But when we discover that the "me," the "I" is the same as the image, then what takes place? You understand my question? Before, you made an effort to get rid of it; the effort came from the "me," who said, "I must get rid of it." Now what will you do? You understand the question?

I DON'T TELL you. I don't tell you anything. I say to you right from the beginning, let us in all our discussions, in all our dialogues, say, "Don't accept anything from the speaker." Right? I am not your authority, I am not your guru; you are not my followers. I say, let's together investigate the problem: What is right action in relationship? The right action cannot take place in relationship when there is any kind of hurt. Who is hurt? You are investigating, not accepting what I am saying. Who is hurt? We said, the image. Is the image different from "me"? And we said, the image is created by thought and the "me" is created by thought also. Am I going too fast?

Questioner: Why do I think I am an image?

K: Aren't you the image? Have you got a name, a form, all the psychological structure, the content? When you say, "I must be better, I am not good, I must be taller, my hair is not right," the whirlpool that is going on all the time, isn't all that your image about yourself? And is yourself different from you who are looking at it?

NOW LOOK! YOU look at me—don't you?—because, unhappily, I am sitting on a platform, you look at me. Right? Have you an image about me?

Q: Yes.

K: Then you are looking at the image, aren't you, which you have built about me? So you put a mask on me and are looking at the mask. Right?

Q: That creates a lot of conflict.

K: Yes, sir. So remove the mask and you will see me, if you can. Right? So if the image is the "me" then what takes place?

Q: To remove the mask . . .

K: That's an image. Drop it, don't take it too seriously. You understand my question? Answer my question: If you are the image, what has happened? Is the hurt there? Is the conflict there between the "me" and the image? What takes place? Before there was an illusion that "me" is different from the image, but suddenly that illusion has gone, and only the fact remains. What is that that remains?

Q: The real you.

K: What is the real you?

Q: I'd say a real illusion.

K: What is the real you? You have suddenly introduced a new word—the real you. This is a trick played by the ancient Hindus, which has been knocked on the head everlastingly. But we still carry on—not that you are a Hindu, or Buddhist, but this sense that there is something behind. So I am asking you what remains, what is there when you realize, or when you have an insight, when you really understand—to understand implies no illusion—when all that isn't there, what is there then? Careful, careful! No you are missing something; go slowly!

Q: There is a whole, one unit.

K: There is the whole. What do you mean by that? Do you mean there is sanity? Right? Which means there is no fragmentation. Right? Careful. Look what you are saying, observe it, don't just spin it out, but watch it carefully. There is no fragmentation between the "me" and the image, which are two fragments. So there is no fragmentation; therefore there is sanity. You are saying where there is sanity there is no fragmentation. So you are sane, therefore there is no insanity in you as a person. So I am asking you—don't let's accept the word *whole* yet—I am asking you, what is there? You understand? We said that the name, the form and the psychological content of the image, all that is the "me" and the image. Right? What is that? The name, the form, the content, are they not just words? Are they not just memories? Are they not some things that you have remembered, past experiences? Is not all that the past?

Q: I think that is all it is, because that is a fact.

K: So apart from your organic biological thing, what are you? Just a lot of words, memories?

Q: It seems like it.

K: Not, "seems like it," is it so? If it is so, if that is the truth, then how can words affect other words? You follow? You understand? Therefore you are completely free, except biologically. You don't see it!

Q: Physical things may hurt me but names will not.

K: Words will not.

Q: If there is no "I."

K: That's right; there is no "I," therefore nothing can hurt you. Which doesn't mean you have become callous, indifferent; on the contrary, you may become much more compassionate, tremendously affectionate. Right?

So what is right action then? If there is an image between you and me, there is disorder in our relationship. Right? You talked about order, you wanted order. How can there be order in our relationship if we are constantly at battle with each other because the images are fighting? So there can only be order when there is no image. And when there is no image, in our relationship there is right action. You don't have to say, "Well, what is right action," there is right action. You have understood it?

Q: What is that which is doing the right action?

K: No, there is right action, not, "Who is it that is doing right action?"

Q: What is doing the right action?

Q: Are we just a bag of protoplasm?

K: I don't quite understand.

Q: What is carrying out the action, the right action?

K: I get it! What do you think? Don't shrug your shoulders. You understand this is a very important question. And we have gone into it very deeply, if you have gone with it, shared it together. We said, we are name, form, and psychological content, you follow, all that. Memories, brain, I remember my name, I identify the name with the form, and the name and the form carry on to the psychological thing, and they are the content of all that. All that is me, the image. Now what is all that, apart from the biological structure and nature and activity, which has, if one observes carefully, its own intelligence. That is, we have destroyed the organic intelligence. We have destroyed it by drink, by giving in to taste: "I like that, it tastes better, therefore I am used to that." Gradually we have destroyed the biological, instinctive intelligence.

Now we are saying, psychologically we have destroyed the deeper intelligence. Let me go into it slowly, slowly. I am investigating. Don't accept what I am saying. Right? We are investigating, we are sharing together. I am saying all that psychological content is the "me" and the image. Isn't that content memories, past experience, knowledge, words, the past? Now when there is the realization that the whole thing is put together by thought, thought being the response of the past.... Now, let's stop there. What is thought?

Q: It's as you said, it's all from the past.

K: What is thought?

Q: A movement in time.

Q: The actual brain trying to balance itself.

K: Now just a minute. I ask you what your name is. You answer very quickly, don't you? Why?

Q: The memory responds.

K: Go slowly. I ask you what your name is and you answer very quickly, don't you? Why?

Q: You are familiar with it.

K: She says, you are familiar with it, you have repeated it a hundred million times. So immediately you answer. Just a minute, go slowly, go slowly. I ask you what the distance is between here and London. What takes place?

Q: It takes longer.

K: What do you mean by longer?

Q: It takes you a certain amount of time.

K: I know. What is happening in your mind?

Q: You are searching in your memory.

K: Slowly. What is happening in your mind, in your brain?

Q: Thinking it out.

K: Thinking, what does that mean?

Q: You are searching out the right information.

K: Yes, thought is searching out information. Right? In a book, or trying to remember how many miles it is, or waiting for somebody to tell you. Right? You follow this? So I ask you, what is the distance between here and London, and thought is immediately active, it says, "I have heard it, I have forgotten it, let me think for a minute. I don't know, but I will find out, I will ask somebody, I will look in that book." So thought is movement, searching in its own memory, or looking somewhere to find out. So thought is in action. Right? Are you sure?

Now I ask you something else. I ask you a question to which you say, "I really don't know," which means what? You are not searching, thought is not in movement. Thought then says, "I don't know, I can't answer you." You see the difference? Familiarity and quick answer—the time interval when thought is searching, looking, asking, expecting, and thought says, when you ask a question that it really doesn't know, that it can't answer from any book, it says, "I don't know." Thought stops there. You understand? See the difference. Quick response because you are familiar, time interval when thought is in operation, and a question that nobody can answer when thought says, "I don't know." Thought is then blocked.

So what is thinking? I have said it to you, come on.

Q: Thought is the response of memory.

K: Memory is what?

Q: Symbols.

K: Symbols, pictures, information—right? Pictures. We said thought is the response of memory. What is memory?

Q: Knowledge.

K: Knowledge, experience stored up in the brain. So the brain retains the experience, the knowledge of how many miles there are between here and London, and responds. Right? So you have found out something: that thought is a response or movement of memory. When I learn how to drive a car, it is the response of knowledge, which is stored up, and I drive. So thought has created the image and because thought is a fragment it has created the "me," thinking the two are different. Thought has created the image, and thought says, "The image is very transient, it is always changing, but there is a 'me' that is permanent." Thought has created both. Right? So when thought sees this, that it has created both and therefore they are both the same, what happens?

Q: Thought stops.

K: Thought is blocked, isn't it? It says, "I can't do anything." No? So what is there? You understand? Please understand this tremendously important thing in your life. For God's sake understand this. Get the principle of it, the truth of it, see the fact of it. Thought has created the image, thought has created the "me," and thought says now, "I have created the battle between the two." Right? And thought suddenly says, "By Jove, I see what I have done." Then what takes place?

Q: You don't think about it.

K: There is no image at all. When thought stops, what is there? There is no illusion, there is no image, there is no "me"; therefore there is no hurt, and therefore out of that comes right action, which is intelligent. Intelligence says, "This is right action." You understand this? Intelligence doesn't *say* it, intelligence *is* right action.

Q: Don't you need thought for intelligence?

K: On the contrary! I have just shown it to you. Please listen carefully. Listen, not to your opinions, not to your conclusions, not to what you have understood, just listen, find out. We said thought is the response of memory. Right? Thought has created the whole psychological structure, the "me" and the image, the image that says, "I am good," "I am bad," "I am superior," and so on. And thought also has created the "me," and says, "I am much more lasting, I will endure death," and so on. So thought has created both. You come along and say, "Look at it carefully. Thought has created both, so they are both the same. There is no division between the 'I' and the image. There is no division between the observer and the observed. There is no division between the thinker and the thought. There is no division between the experiencer and the experience." Sorry I am ramming all this into you.

So suddenly thought realizes how perfectly true this is. It is true; thought doesn't *realize* it, it *is* true. Right? The perception of the truth is intelligence, and that intelligence then says, "Whatever I do is right action." Because there is no image, there is no "me," there is no psychological content, only intelligence operating. Do you get this?

Q: If thought has stopped, or is blocked, then it is obvious that you don't use thought for your . . .

K: . . . except to drive a car, to use a language, to do technical functions, and so on. There is no psychological content. You understand this is a tremendous thing to discover for yourself. Therefore you can live a life without conflict, therefore live a life with tremendous compassion and all the rest of it.

Q: I have the impression of using thought to discover all this.

K: No, we are using words to convey the meaning, which thought has created. Look! I describe something to you; the description is the movement of thought. Right? The description is the movement of thought, but the description is not the described. The described is not thought. The tree is not thought, but I have described it. Get it?

So what is left is complete freedom from the image and "me." You understand? This is what all the saints, the serious ones, and what all the great teachers have sought, so as to be in a state where there is only intelligence operating, which is the intelligence of perception of truth. Have you understood all this? Have you got an insight into it? Not a verbal description, you understand?

Q: Is that why we call it "holiness"?

K: That is holy. That intelligence is sacred, not the things created by the hand or by the mind, the statues, the temples, the churches. That's not holy, it is the product of thought. The architect who had an image as a design and put it down on paper and then built it, is all thought. That's a reality, you follow? This building has been put together by the architect and it's a reality, it is so, it is there. But the "I," the image is not there.

Q: What is the difference between reality and the "I"?

K: Look at the organism; are you the body?

Q: Yes.

K: You are? What do you mean by that?

Q: Two arms, two legs.

K: Yes, and the name Jean-Michel, the form, the shape of the head, the shape of the eyes, the shape of the nose, the height and breadth, right? That's a reality. The organism is a reality, but the psychological thing that thought has created is not a reality. Wait, wait, go slowly. The body, the organism, the biological structure is not the creation of thought. The tree is not the creation of thought. Right? Now thought has created the psychological structure. That's also a reality. Wait! But it is an illusion.

Q: Is the illusion in the fact that you don't realize it is created by thought?

K: Of course. Is not illusion created by thought, all illusions: I believe in the perfect State, perfect government, that the Communists have the most perfect organizing capacity, and so on. I believe. That's an illusion, but what they do is a reality. Have you got it? If I disagree with them, they send me to a mental hospital. The hospital and me in the hospital are reality, but it is brought about by an illusion.

So we are going to find out. That is, whatever thought has created is a reality. Thought says, "I am Napoleon"; it is an illusion, but I think it is a fact. You understand? But the tree is not an illusion, it is a fact; it is not created by thought. So intelligence is not created by thought.

Q: That's what I was saying. If your thought stops, how could it be.

K: Therefore it is intelligence that operates when there is a relationship that is not based on images. Right? Then that intelligence in relationship brings right action. Got it? You have understood a little bit of it? Hold on to the tail of the tiger, don't let it go, because you will see that if you hold on you will enter into quite a different dimension. But if you let go it is like coming back to living with the beastly life of struggle and conflict and battle with each other. You understand?

Saanen, 20 July 1976

THE PROBLEM OF consciousness is very complex. The content of consciousness is the whole nature and structure of consciousness. One is only aware of that consciousness of oneself when one has any kind of problem, strife, contradiction, anger, jealousy, and so on; it is only then that one becomes completely conscious of oneself. Otherwise there is no consciousness of the "me."

I think it is important to talk over together the question of suffering, and the word *love*, which has been so misused, and what the real significance or meaning of that word is. To go into these questions rather deeply, one has to begin with what we call relationship, human relationship. Otherwise love becomes an abstraction without much meaning and remains something printed in a book, or talked about in a church or a temple, and then completely forgotten.

To put it very, very simply we should begin I think by pointing out that relationship is the whole structure of society. This is a very complex problem. But to inquire into that question one must begin very near; that is, very near, our human relationship with each other. Then discover from there what right relationship is, if there is such a thing, and move from there to the question of what the nature of love is, whether love can exist as long as human beings suffer, and if there is an end to suffering, especially psychologically. So we are going to go into this very complex problem.

As we said, we have to begin very near to find out actually what our relationship is with each other. On that our whole social, moral, ethical structure is based. That is society, the society that we have built, a society that is at present utterly immoral, degraded, destructive. If we would change the social structure this must begin from within, not merely change from outside. I think that is fairly obvious as one observes more and more the attempts made by Communists and other reformers; they think that by altering, reshaping the social, environmental structure, human beings will radically change. And when one examines the various experiments made in India in ancient times, and in China in recent times, basically human beings don't change even though the environment changes. It is very important, it seems to me, that we should understand the relationship of ourselves to society, and whether in transforming the human mind and consciousness basically, a new social order can come into being. That is one of our problems, because social order must change inevitably. There must be radical transformation of it. The terrorists, the revolutionaries, and the idealists, some of them at least, think that by changing the environment, throwing bombs and all the rest of the physical revolution, it will somehow transform the nature and the structure of human consciousness. We think that the radical transformation of society can take place only when there is a radical transformation in human consciousness. I think we have made that very clear from the beginning.

So we must find out what our human relationship is to society, human relationship with each other, human relationship with the whole of humanity, a global relationship. So what is, actually, in our daily life, our relationship to each other, and what is it based on? As we said, the word is not the thing, the description is not the described. What we are doing now is a verbal description, but if we are caught in the description and don't go to the described, the fact, then we will merely skim the surface and it will lose all meaning. So one must be aware, conscious, or whatever word one may use, not to be caught in words, not to be caught in descriptions, conclusions, but rather to look at, observe what actually is our relationship in daily life, and whether that relationship can be transformed into something other than "what is." That is our question. To transform "what is" one must be concerned and observe completely "what is," and not imagine "what should be." Right?

What is our relationship based on? Is it on knowledge? Is it on experience? Is it on various forms of intellectual, emotional, sentimental conclusions? Please, as we are saying, observe, if you do not mind, your own actual relationship with another—actual, not what you think it ought to be, not an ideal relationship, but factual, daily, everyday relationship—because that is what we live with, and if we understand that then we can go much further. But without delving deeply into that, merely to imagine, or have a fanciful relationship has no meaning, because we are dealing with facts, and not with ideational abstractions that would lead nowhere. So what is our relationship actually?

Relationship means to respond. The root meaning of that word, not what we have made of that word, is to respond completely to another, like responsibility. Do we ever respond totally with each other, or is it always a fragmentary response, a partial response? If it is a partial, fragmentary response, why is it? You understand my questions? I hope we are communicating with each other because this is really very important. Like everything else that we have talked about, human relationship is one of the most radical, basic, essential things that we have to find out about, because from that we may find out for ourselves what love is, what love *really* is, not what we have made of it. So it is most important for each one of us to find out what our relationships actually are, whether they can be transformed, and if it is possible to transform them radically.

Is not our relationship based on memory, memory piled up through various emotional, irrational, or sexual responses? That is, there is desire plus thought, and thought creates the image. Right? Desire, that is sensation, plus thought, and thought creates the image of myself and of you. So there are two images: myself and that which I have made out of you. Right? Go into it with me, please. This is your life and for heaven's sake give some thought to this thing, because we are destroying each other; we are destroying the earth, the air—everything we touch we have destroyed. And I think we do not feel utterly responsible for all this. So please give your attention, which means your care, your affection, to find out what our relationships actually are.

We said our relationship is sensation plus thought, which is desire, and the image that thought has shaped according to that desire. So I have an image about myself, various images, the business image, the intellectual image, the emotional image, and various images that society has helped me to build, education has helped me to build. *I* have an image, and my relationship with *you* is another image that I am making of you. Right? That is an absolute fact. The image, or the picture, or the form, is you, and I am related to you through that picture. I am attached to that picture. As you are my wife, my friend, my girl or boy, or whatever, I am attached to the image that I have made about you, and I am holding to that image. And that image is projected through the various incidents in our contact with each other. And you have an image about yourself, various images, and you add me as another image. So your image and my image of you are related.

Go into this, please go into this. Look at yourself. You may have been married for five or ten years, or you have a girlfriend or a boyfriend, and slowly the images are built, consciously or unconsciously, generally unconsciously. So the image has taken root through nagging, through domination, through assertions, insults, possessiveness, attachments—you follow? All those incidents have built this image in me of you. And you do the same about me. This we call relationship, and this we call love. "I love you," which is, I love the image that I have built of you. It sounds rather cynical, but it is not; this is actual fact.

So why does the brain build such images? Do you understand my question? I have built one about you, and you have built one about me. This is a fact and I am asking: Why does the brain do this? Which is, thought, why does thought create this division between you and me through the image? Is that clear? Why?

As we said, the brain needs security. From childhood, children need security, they must be protected. We don't protect them, but that's another matter. We destroy them. That is another issue. So the brain needs complete security. It may find security in an illusion, God, fanciful images, all kinds of things and therefore be neurotic. Or it may find security in the image that it has built as knowledge. You are following this? So the brain has made this image through thought, to be completely secure. I *know* my wife—you follow?—I *know* her. A positive assertion. That is, the image that I have built about her gives me that feeling that I have her completely, she is mine. And the other way round, and so on, and so on. So the images are built through the desire to be completely secure. That is one of the factors.

And having an image is very convenient, because you don't then have to look at her, or him; you don't have to bother. You feel utterly responsible to that image, not to the human being. Watch yourself, please! And having an image of each other, you live your daily life at a very superficial level, the superficial level being sexual. And one goes off to the office and comes back; you know this very superficial life that one lives. That is one of the reasons why the images become tremendously important.

Now when one becomes aware of this process of the image-maker and the image, when one becomes conscious of this, then one asks: Can the image making stop? You understand my question? This is very important. Please look at yourself, look at your relationship. You have an image and I have an image, and our relationships are based on that.

The next question is: Why does the brain find some reason for doing it? And another question is: Is it possible not to make an image at all? If that can be prevented then our relationship becomes tremendously significant. Are we meeting each other? We are asking: Is it possible not to build the image? The image-maker is thought, obviously. Right? Thought is time, the remembrance of many incidents of yesterday, which is time, and through time the image has been formed, day after day, day after day. Thought has built the image through desire, sensation, and so on. Now we are asking whether this whole momentum, which is the momentum of tradition, can stop.

We are slaves to tradition. We may think we are modern, very free, but deep down we are very traditional, which you can see when we accept this image making and establish our relationship with each other on those images. This is as ancient as the hills. That is one of our traditions. We accept it, live with it, torture each other with it. So can that tradition come to an end? That is, when an incident within our relationship takes place, a happening, not register it at all? Have you understood? No.

In our daily relationship you say something in anger, in irritation, and the brain registers it and adds to the image that it has already built about you. Can that insult, that irritation, that anger at something that you said, which hurt me, hurt the image, can that stop? You understand my question? It can stop only when you understand the whole process of registration. The brain registers everything. It is now registering what I am saying. And when an incident takes place it is registered. Now we are saying, can that registration stop? You understand this question? I insult you in our relationship, and immediately reaction takes place, which is the registration. Now can that end? Because otherwise our love is merely emotional, sentimental, sexual, and rather superficial. It is only a mind that is not hurt that is capable of loving, isn't it? You see the meaning of it? Come on, please. So you hurt me, which is, you hurt my image that I have built about myself. Can that insult not be registered at all so that my brain is not hurt? Then I will know the full meaning and the beauty of something that I have felt exists but only now realize. So I am going to find out whether it is possible to stop that hurt being registered at all.

It is possible only when the image is *not*. Is that clear? When I have no image about you and you have no image about me, it is only then that whatever you say leaves no mark. This doesn't mean I am isolated, or I have no affection, but the registration of hurts, insults, all those movements of thought, have come to an end. Which is, at the moment of insult to be completely attentive, with all your senses. You see, our *brains* are hurt. Through various shocks, incidents, a sense of tremendous damage is being done to the brain. It wants security, therefore it finds security in normal and abnormal things. Like a nation, the worship of a nation is abnormal, a tribal instinct, but it finds security there, and so on, and so on. The very desire to be secure is destroying it. You understand? I am secure with my family. With my family there is a battle going on all the time, between me and you, with my children, constant conflict, agony, despair, annoyance. You know all that is going on day after day, day after day. That is a great shock to the brain. And so we are saying: As long as there is an image-maker there must be hurts, there must be registration. It is only when the image-maker is not that no registration takes place. Which means there is no "me" who is the image that gets hurt. You understand? There is no "me." "Me" is the image that I have about myself as an extraordinarily capable or successful human being, the things that thought has built around itself as the me, the deep conscious or unconscious image that it has built.

In our relationship the image making becomes an extraordinary everyday activity and therefore there is actually no relationship. Relationship can only take place when there is no image. Do you understand what I am saying? Have you got something of this? Not verbally, but *actually*, in your blood! Then it brings a truth into our relationship.

So then what is our relationship if there is no image between you and me? When you actually have no image about me, then what is your relationship to me? When you have no image, and I have an image, then what takes place between us? Because I have an image about myself I am in a battle with you; you have no image, therefore you are not in a battle with me. You understand? Can you, in our relationship, bring about in me a state of mind in which the image making has ended? That's your responsibility to me. When you have no image, and I have an image about you, you have the responsibility in our relationship to see that I don't make images about you. That is your responsibility. Then you are watching, you are alert, you are fully alive, and I am half asleep all my life. So it is your responsibility to see that I have no image.

So two people having no image—if it ever takes place—is a most miraculous thing, greater than any miracle in the world. If that takes place, then there is a totally different kind of communion with each other. Which means never quarrelling—do you understand?—never being possessive, never dominating, never shaping each other by words, threats, innuendo. Then we have a relationship of the most extraordinary kind. I know it can take place. It has been done, we have done it. It is not just a lot of words.

We are saying, when there is no image then there is love. So we have to find out what that love is actually. What is it that we call love now in our life? When you say you love somebody, what does it mean? Is it sexual love, a biological affair, and the memory of it, the demand for it, the pursuit of it? It apparently has an extraordinary significance in our life, is blown up in every magazine, in every cinema, and all the rest of it. Is it sexual love? Is it love when there is jealousy? You understand? Is there love when—please listen—when I go off to the office or factory, or become a secretary, or whatever I do, and you do something else also because you want to fulfil yourself. The wife wants to fulfil herself, and the husband wants to fulfil himself, and the children want to fulfil themselves; so where are we? You understand? So all this is called "love," "responsibility." So to find out what love is, there must be no fragmentation, no fragmentation in my work and the implications of that work, and no division between my work and my family, my wife, my girl. Do you understand what I am saying? It is not broken up. I go to the office; there I am very ambitious, greedy, and envious, desiring success, you know, pushing, pushing, driving, competing, and then I come home and say, "Oh, darling I love you." It all becomes so cheap. And that is our tradition.

So we are asking: Is it possible to live a life that is totally harmonious, whole, so that when I go to the office I am still whole there, not something different from my family? You understand? Is that possible? Don't say it is an idea, it is utopian. One has to make it possible, one has to work at this thing, put your teeth into it to find out, because we are destroying ourselves.

Love comes into being only when there is total harmony in oneself, in whatever action one is doing, and so there is no conflict between the outer and the inner. To find out how to live that way, how to live a life that is not contradictory, that is not broken up, that is not convenient, comfortable, that is total, whole, harmonious, to find that out one must go into the question of sorrow. They are all related, you understand? Relationship, love, and sorrow; they are all interrelated.

Man has lived with this thing called sorrow. From antiquity man has carried this burden. And we are still carrying that burden; we are very sophisticated, highly technical and so on, but inwardly there is this grief, this ache, this loneliness, this sense of isolation, this sense of the great burden of sorrow, not only the sorrow of one's own little life, but the sorrow of humanity. Are we meeting each other? The sorrow of humanity, sirs: they are suffering in India, in Asia, in the Arab world, in the Jewish world, in Russia; human beings are suffering, there is global suffering. And our little selves are also suffering. So we are asking: Is it possible to end that suffering? If there is no end to suffering then there is no compassion, then there is no love, then there is no relationship. This is what is actually happening in our society: no relationship, no love, no compassion, no ending of sorrow; therefore we are making a hideous mess of our lives. Do you understand?

So we are asking: Is there an end to sorrow? This is a question that every human being has asked when he is at all serious, when he has looked at his own sorrow and the sorrow of another. He asks this question: "Can it ever end? Or is there an everlasting misery of man?" We are going to find out, not in abstraction, not as a theory, but actually find out if you, as a human being who represents the world, and the world is you, whether you can end that sorrow. We are going to find out.

This is a very serious matter, like everything else in life, and very complex. To find out what love is one has to shed every tradition, every sense of emotion, sentiment, all the things that one has built round oneself, to put away all that. Then, to come upon something that is whole, total, harmonious, one has to work, look, observe. So we are going to do the same with sorrow.

There is a biological pain, a physical pain, and that pain is registered in the mind, in the brain. There is the fear that it might happen again tomorrow, and that brings sorrow also. There is loneliness, deep isolation, feeling unrelated to everything in life, and the sense of complete withdrawal, complete sense of nothing to which the mind can be related. And that is a tremendous sorrow. I do not know if you have known this. Most human beings do. Then there is the sorrow of death. You have lost the person and you are left behind; the loneliness, the sudden cessation of that person whom you thought you loved, cared for, had companionship with, in whom perhaps you may have invested all your immortality, all that. There is sorrow there too. And there is the sorrow of all the people in the world who have been killed in so-called wars of religion, wars of nationality, wars of security, killing millions and millions for your own particular nation, for your own particular security. There is all that immense untold sorrow. You understand all this? And we are responsible for all this, not the Americans in Vietnam, or the Arabs in Beirut; human beings are responsible for this, because their primary demand is: please give me security. And the security takes the form of nationality, the form of religious beliefs that go very deep. You hold on to that; that is your security, for which you are willing to kill and destroy. All that has brought about thousands of years of sorrow. Right? We are describing this; please don't get emotional about it because this is what we have to face and to understand.

So there is this sorrow of man. Can it end? If it doesn't end we are chained everlastingly to this misery. The suffering may be conscious or unconscious. So we have to look at the unconscious, the deep down, the hidden, as well as the conscious. And this means we have to go back into the question of what is consciousness.

The Western world, through Freud and others, has divided consciousness into the unconscious and the conscious. The unconscious is racial, communal, inherited, tradition, memories, motives. And the conscious is the highly sophisticated, educated, technical mind. So there is a division between the conscious and the unconscious. Right? That is your tradition. It may not be like that at all. What has divided it? Thought—right? Unless we understand the deep meaning of the movement of thought, every movement it makes must be divisive. So in the deep layers of one's consciousness is there sorrow? Is there the sorrow of thousands of years of human suffering, stored up, brought from the past to the present in a human being, deep down in the very deep recesses of one's mind? We said that is part of the content of consciousness. The part makes the whole. The past is consciousness. So there is in us the past suffering of man as well as the present suffering of man, in our consciousness. Can that thing end? Do you see the importance of its ending, the essentiality of it? Don't accept it and say, "Well it has been going on for a million years, what about it, a few more people suffering, a few people not suffering, what importance does it have?" It has tremendous importance because when a human being transforms himself totally, radically, then he affects the whole of the consciousness of man. You understand? I'll show it to you.

Isn't your consciousness affected by all the things of the past, by Hitler, by Stalin, by all the tyrannies, by all the brutalities? All that is the past. The content of that consciousness is the human consciousness. You are affected, as you are living in the Western world, by Christianity. That Christianity, put together by priests, is part of your consciousness.

So suffering is part of this consciousness, whether hidden or whether one is aware of it. Now we are asking if all that immense burden of loneliness, despair, isolation, withdrawal through various forms of hurts, building a resistance around oneself can come to an end, not gradually, not over years, but end now? You understand my question? You understand what I am saying? We are used to, we have been trained, educated, it is our habit, to say, "Well I will do it gradually. It may take time but I will do it." Which is, I am suffering now, gradually I will end suffering. There is that vast gap between the ending and the beginning. And in that gap various other forms of incidents and accidents take place, therefore there is always postponement. You are following all this? Therefore one has to break down this tradition of eventuality.

We are asking if that sorrow, which is part of human conditioning, part of our consciousness, can end, not in some distant happy future, but *now?* The now is the most important—you understand? So find out what that now is, so that it ends? The now is the past meeting the present, and if the past meeting the present modifies itself and goes to the future, then there is no now. That is, the past, my memories, my anxieties, my hopes, my remembrances, pleasures, pains, all that is a movement with the present. That is, I meet you, there is the challenge of the present and it modifies itself and proceeds to the future. So time is a movement from the past, through the present to the future. This is what we are accustomed to, this is part of our tradition. The Communists say, thesis, antithesis, and synthesis, which is bit by bit, bit by bit. So the past meeting the present, modified, proceeds further to the future. We are saying that the now is when the past meets the present and ends that movement. It can only end when you know the whole structure of memory, as experience, as knowledge, and the response of that knowledge, experience, and memory, which is thought; when thought brings the past to the present, for thought to end it there and not proceed to tomorrow. I wonder if you capture all this. Get this, because it is very important for your life so that there is an ending all the time.

So when you are feeling lonely, isolated, in great sorrow on the death of another, or on losing a job, and so on, and so on—the different sorrows that human beings have created for themselves—to face that loneliness. It is brought about by the self-centred activity of daily life. That loneliness is the synthesis, the essence of our daily self-centred activity. To face that loneliness and not give it a future. That is, to look at it, to observe it completely, with all your senses, with complete attention, then you will see that the past meets the present and ends it, so that there is no future to loneliness; it has ended. In the same way end sorrow, with which you are quite familiar, for most of us have built various escapes from that—escapes through church, through reading books, you know, a dozen ways. The very escape from sorrow only strengthens it, obviously. So, to be aware of the escapes, which means giving it time to flower, to be aware of the escapes and by meeting that suffering completely, without any sense of distortion by thought, then there is an ending to suffering.

Only when there is an ending to suffering is there compassion. The word *suffering* is related to compassion. Compassion means passion for *all* things. You understand? For all things. That means no killing. But Christians are used to killing. They have probably killed more people than anybody else. So no killing, which means to live on things that you have to kill like vegetables—you *have* to kill, you understand?—but not to kill animals. When there is this sense of compassion then you don't kill a thing, by word, by gesture, by an idea.

So what we are saying is: In the understanding of relationship, love comes into being. And in the understanding of love we alter the structure of society, and there is an ending to sorrow. It is only then there is compassion. You know compassion is the most extraordinary thing in life, because there is no "me" who is compassionate. There is only that state of compassion that is not mine or yours.

Saanen, 31 July 1977

WE ARE TALKING about something very important, it seems to me at least. We are asking: What is love in relationship with each other, the love that exists between man and woman, the love of a mother with her baby, the love of one's country, and so on? Can there be love if there is no total comprehension or self-knowledge? And there is also the question: What is the relationship between human beings who have self-knowledge, or who understand themselves?

WHAT IS THE relationship between human beings—man, woman, husband, wife, mother and baby, and so on? Because if our relationship is not correct—I am using the word *correct* in the sense of actual, truthful, right—then we create a society that is disintegrating, appalling, or a world of totalitarianism. We create it and accept it.

It is very important to understand relationship. The meaning of the word is to be related, actually to be related, to be in contact, to have empathy, sympathy, a sensitivity that understands each other completely, not partially. As most human beings do not have that relationship at all, their relationship is based on conflict. How does this conflict arise? Please this is important; let us go together into this because our life is involved. Don't let's waste our life, we have got only this life. Whatever the future life may be, if we don't change what we are now, we will continue in a different form—I won't go into that.

It is very important to understand this question of relationship because that is part of self-knowledge, part of knowing oneself. Through the understanding of relationship, which is the outside, you can then move inwardly. Are we related at all to anything, to nature, each other? In our private, intimate, sexual relationship, the mother and the baby, and so on, what is this relationship based on? Please follow it for yourself. You have your husband, your girlfriend, or boyfriend, are a mother with a baby, all that is part of our life. So please follow, if you will, be serious for once in your life.

What is this relationship based on? Is it two entities, two human beings deeply concerned with themselves, deeply occupied with their own ambitions, with their own worries, with their own anxieties, uncertainties, confusion, these two people meeting—a boy and a girl, and so on, and so on. Then there is all the problem of sex, and because in this relationship each is separate inwardly there is conflict. Obviously. Right? Can we go on with it?

So conflict becomes inevitable when each one of us is occupied so entirely with himself; which we are. In exploring this, we need to be tremendously honest; otherwise the game is not worth playing. Now the problem is: Can this relationship exist without effort, without this constant strife between human beings, and what then is that relationship in which there is no conflict at all? Why does this conflict exist at all? It seems that this conflict exists because each one is centred within himself; from himself he goes out, from himself he acts, from himself he says, "I love you," but the centre is the "me," the self. This is clear, isn't it? We are describing what is very obvious.

Now the question is: Can that centre be understood and dissolved? Otherwise life, which is relationship, must inevitably be a series of incidents and conflicts. That's clear. So we are asking: Can this centre be understood, watched; can the nature, the structure of it be seen, and ended, not verbally but *actually* ended? That is our question. Therefore one must observe freely the nature and the structure of the self.

So various questions are put: "What am I; who am I?," and looking at what the latest psychologist with his peculiar ideas and new ways of thinking says, you say, "By Jove, I will accept that." We are saying don't accept anything because then you are merely copying what the psychologist says you are. So there is no authority in the observation of oneself. Wipe out Freud, Jung, and the whole bally lot of them and begin, because then what you discover is original, not secondhand. Right?

Ojai, 21 April 1979

AN EXCELLENT ARCHITECT has acquired a great deal of knowledge, he has built many houses, cathedrals, halls, and so on. That knowledge has been accumulated, he has read, he has worked at it, he has had experience with various types of houses, halls, and so on. So with that knowledge he builds houses. There knowledge is necessary, obviously. But psychological knowledge, the knowledge that I want this, that I have experienced this, I believe this, this is my opinion, all that, the psychological residue of one's experiences, and the experiences of mankind stored up in the brain, from that there is thought and that thought is always and ever limited. And any action born from that must inevitably be limited and therefore not harmonious, but contradictory, divisive, conflicting, and so on.

So psychologically, thought itself may be the root of disorder. You understand the beauty, the fun, and also the logic of it? So then one asks: Has thought any place in relationship? You understand? Is our relationship with each other, being intimate or superficial, being in contact physically, emotionally, intellectually, based on thought? We are asking this question, together exploring this with the same mind to find out. If our relationship is based on thought, which is on remembrance, then our relationship must be limited. Obviously. Therefore in that limitation there is contradiction, you and I, me and you, my opinion, my ambition, you are not responding to my sexual demands, but opposing me, and so on.

Please, this is serious because we are going to inquire into the nature of love. Because this basic thing has to be understood, which is, desire, thought, then order. The very essence of love is order. We will go into it.

If thought, being limited, creates disorder, as desire does, then what place has thought in our relationship; not in walking, talking, driving a car, building a house, earning money, shelter, clothes, but in our relationship, man and woman, what place has thought? Please inquire, go into it with me together, don't wait for me to tell you. If thought is the ruling factor in our relationship then, thought being limited, our relationship must be very, very limited and therefore contradictory, opposing, destructive. So is our relationship based on thought, on remembrance? Of course it is, if you are honest. So then one asks: Is love merely a remembrance, a sexual remembrance? Is love the remembrance of a pleasure? For God's sake please pay attention to all this, it's your life. The way the word *love* is used in this country is so meaningless.

We are asking together because we have the same mind to find out, because this may bring about order in our lives; then we may be able to live with an extraordinary sense of happiness. Happiness is not pleasure, it is order. With order comes freedom, and with freedom there is responsibility. So we are asking: Is love a remembrance, is love desire, is love pleasure, is love attachment? And if it is a remembrance in which there is attachment, then there is anxiety, conflict, jealousy, anger, hatred. Right? And all this you call love. Right?

WE ARE ASKING together: Is love merely a fulfilment of desire? You understand? Desire we explained very carefully. Is love the pursuit of pleasure? Which is what you all want. And if it is based on remembrance then there is a contradiction; it is limited, therefore it is disastrous in our relationship and therefore we will create a society that is utterly destructive. You see, we are saying love is not desire, love is not the pursuit of pleasure, love is not a remembrance; it is something entirely, totally different. That sense of love, which is one of the factors of compassion, comes only when you begin to understand the whole movement of desire, the whole movement of thought. Then out of that depth of understanding, feeling, a totally different thing called love comes into being. It may not be the thing that *we* call love. It is totally a different dimension.

Brockwood Park, 2 September 1979

A PROBLEM ARISES when our relationships, whether intimate or impersonal, are not understood. Why have we not understood relationship and seen the depth of it? Apparently we have never resolved this problem. You know all about it, don't you? Why? Is it that you love, but you are not loved? Is that a problem? Come on, it is a problem. Or you don't love and the other does. Or in your relationship with another you are possessive, you are dominant, dependent, you want something from her or from him, sex, pleasure, comfort. Somebody said to the speaker the other day, "If I leave her, who will wash my clothes?" Do you understand? I wonder if you understand all this?

So what is relationship, out of which we have made such a tremendous problem? Relationship means to be related to another, to one or to many or to the whole of mankind. Oh, you don't see it! Why is there not in this relationship peace, a depth of understanding of each other that brings about love? Why isn't there? The sexual relationship between two people, a man and woman, is called love. Right? For God's sake don't let us be hypocrites, let's face these things! It is called love. Is it love? Or is it the demand for sensory satisfaction, the demand for companionship, the demand that is born out of loneliness, the demand that says, "I cannot be alone. I cannot stand this immense solitude in myself, therefore I must have somebody on whom I can depend psychologically." You need the postman, the porter, and all the rest of it, but why is there this tremendous division psychologically in the relationship between man and woman? Is one aware of this great division between you and another, whom you say you love? Do we have to go into that? Is it necessary? Apparently it is.

Have you noticed that between two people their thinking, their feelings are never the same? One is ambitious, the other is not; one is aggressive, the other is not; one is possessive, the other is not; one is dominant and the other is docile. Which means what? Each one is self-centred in his activity. Right? Are you following? Observe yourself. You are self-centred in yourself and the other too is self-centred, so there is division. Where there is division there must be quarrels, there must be antagonism, there must be all kinds of things going on between nationalities. When there is division, there is chaos. And this division we call "love." You don't face it.

So in inquiring into something beyond time there must be a complete sense of relationship, which can only come about when there is love. Right? Love is not pleasure, obviously. That cheapens it. Love is not desire; love is not the fulfilment of your own sensory demands. Are you following all this?

So without love, do what you will, stand on your head and sit in meditation for the rest of your life cross-legged, put on fancy robes, do anything you like, without that quality there is nothing. So if a person wants to find something beyond time there must be right relationship completely so that no problems exist. And this quality of great affection, love, which is not the result of thought, must exist.

Then we can proceed to find out. See how difficult it is. Because most of us are so indulgent with ourselves, most of us are so petty, so small in our outlook. So your mind must be free from all those self-centred anxious movements. Because that creates the problem, and when the mind has problems it cannot possibly see clearly. The mind that is everlastingly chattering, such a mind is not a quiet mind.

Bombay, 25 January 1981

SOCIETY IS AN abstraction. An abstraction is not a reality. What is a reality is the relationship between man and man. The relationship between man and man has created that which we call society. Man is violent, man is self-centred, man is seeking pleasure, frightened, insecure; in himself he is corrupt and this way of relationship, whether it be intimate or not, has created this so-called society. That is clear, obviously. But we always try to change society, not to change man who creates the society in which he lives. Please, this is simple, clear logic. And the Socialist, Communist, capitalist, and so on, have always tried to change this amorphous, abstract thing called society. But they have never tackled the problem of relationship between man and man. Now can that be changed? That is the whole point. Can your relationship with another, which is intimate, sexual, pleasure seeking, based on the idea that you are separate from another and therefore there is battle between you, can all that psychological structure be transformed? You understand? Are we together in this? Or are you just merely following a verbal structure?

The speaker is not a reformer, a social reformer. He is essentially a religious man. He doesn't belong to any society, to any group of religious cantankerous believing types. He doesn't belong to any country; he has no belief, has no ideology, but is only facing what is going on and seeing whether it is possible to change that radically. If you are now serious enough to go into this, let us walk together, knowing that the individual salvation promised by all this structure of religions has no meaning. The speaker is not offering personal salvation. The speaker is saying that there is an ending to sorrow, there is an ending to conflict between man and man; and so a new kind of society can be born out of that. Are you interested in all this?

Who has created the social structure and who has created the "me," which is essentially the psychological structure? We are asking who is responsible for the actual state of the present world? God has certainly not created this present world, the present structure of society with its wars, appalling cruelty, self-centred action, competition. Certainly God has not created this society, but you, man, have created God in your own image. You are frightened, you want comfort, you want security, a sense of stability, so you have created an idea, a concept called God, whom you worship. You understand the irony, the absurdity of it? God has been created by man.

What is the origin of all this? The origin of nature, the universe, the beginning of all this, who is responsible? Most of us, most of you rather, believe in something that is comforting. Like the origin of a river that begins very slowly with a few trickles of water at the source, and then gathers strength as it goes down the hills, mountains, into the valley as an enormous volume of water going to the sea, what is the origin of all this? Man has always tried to find the origin and is still seeking through telescopes, going to the Moon and Saturn. The Western world is inquiring into all this. To find that out, if you are serious, not just accepting some printed book, requires enormous inquiry and energy. It requires a brain that is extraordinarily active, a brain that is not tethered to any problem. It is only a brain that is free of problems that can solve problems. And to find out—not as an individual—to find out the truth of the origin, one must understand the nature of meditation, the ending of all conflict. Then only can one find the origin; then only can the ground from which all this begins be seen.

Who has created the psychological structure—you understand?—the structure that is called the "me," the "you," "we," and "they"? Who is responsible for this, the agony, the anxiety, the enormous suffering of mankind, not only personal sorrow with all its tears, depression, anxiety, and loneliness, but also who has created this extraordinary world of technology that is advancing at an incredible speed? Who has created this inward feeling, this inward sense of despair, anxiety, sorrow? You understand all this? Who has created all this? If you say it is God, he must be a rather strange God. If you say it is karma, past life, which again means you believe, you are stuck in the idea of individuality—which is non-existent. So if you begin to question, investigate sceptically, never accepting any authority, the Gita, the Upanishads, the Bible, the Koran, and all the rest of it, you have a brain that is free to look.

So we are asking: Who has been responsible for these two states, the psychological structure and also the technological world in which you are living—the computer, the robot, the extraordinarily quick communication, the surgery, the medicine—and the inward state—the greed, the envy, the hatred, the brutality, the violence? These two exist together. Who is responsible for all this? Please ask yourself.

Surely thought is responsible. Thought has created the technological world. Thought has concentrated great energy to go to the moon, thought has created rapid communication, thought has created the computer and the robot. So thought has created the technological world. Thought has also created the pictures, the paintings, the poems, the language that we speak. Thought has created the marvellous architecture—perhaps not in Bombay—the great cathedrals, marvellous mosques, the great temples of India, the sculptures; thought has done all that. Thought has also created war. It has divided people as Hindus and Muslims. I hope you are following all this. This division into nationality, which is poison, has been created by thought. The Muslim with his belief, with his dogmas, with his perpetual repetition of something or other, and the Hindu with his conditioning, with his repetition of the Gita and all that stuff, they are both being programmed. Both have been conditioned, the Islamic world for perhaps the last thousand or so years, but the Hindus perhaps for three thousand years. They have been conditioned that way. So thought has created the world outside of us, the technological world, but not nature. Thought has not created the tree, thank God. Thought has not created that marvellous animal the tiger, the gazelle, the river, the ocean, the heavens. But thought has created our psychological world with its fear, anxiety, searching everlastingly for security. It is a fact. The temple has been built by thought, and the thing that is inside the temple is put together by thought; the rituals are created by thought, and all the things that the priest says are created by thought. Right? That is a fact. You might like to say that is sacred, because it has been handed down from generation to generation, but it is still the movement of thought. Thought is not sacred, thought is a material process. This is where our difficulty lies. Thought is a movement in time.

I will go into it; you will see for yourself. Thought is the result or the response of memory. Memory is stored up in the brain; memory is knowledge, knowledge is experience. So experience, knowledge, memory, action, and from that action you learn, which then becomes more knowledge. So man, the brain, is caught in this process: experience, knowledge, memory, thought, action. This is the process in which we all live. Right? There is nothing illogical about this. Thought has created the technological world and thought has created the psychological world, the world of "me": my wife, my husband, my daughter, my ambition, my greed, my envy, my loneliness; despair, sexual appetite, all that is brought about by thought. There is no denying this; it would be absurd to deny it. The guru that you have created is the result of your thought, so you follow what your thought has created. See the absurdity, the immaturity, the childishness of it all. I know it is obvious that you will listen but will go on in your way, because that is the most convenient irrational thoughtless way, and if that is comforting, it indicates that you really don't care what happens in the world; you really don't have any affection, love for mankind. All that you are concerned with is your own little comfort. Right?

But if you want to go into this very deeply we have to inquire into the relationship that thought has established. That relationship has created the society in which we live, a society that is so utterly contradictory—some people making enormous amounts of money and others living in poverty, the wars, the butchery that is going on, and all the rest of it. So to bring about a radical change in society, that society which is an abstraction of the relationship between man and man, it is your relationship with another that has created this monstrous world, that must change. I wonder if one realizes this, not accepting it as an idea but seeing the truth of it, the inwardness of it. How dangerous everything is becoming in the world, overpopulation, communal and national divisions, everything that is going on in the world! This problem cannot be solved by any politician, by any scientist, by any bureaucracy; and no guru will ever solve it. It is only if *you* see this extraordinarily vital thing: that you as a human being are the whole of humanity, and that when you are living just for yourself as an individual, *that* is the most destructive thing, because in that there must be everlasting conflict. If you actually see—not as a theory, not as an idea—the truth that you are psychologically the entire world, entire human being, then you see what happens. It gives you enormous vitality and strength. But the conditioning is so strong—it has been going on for thousands of years—that you are a separate human being. Your religion, your books, everything says that, and if you accept it and live with it you are going to be everlastingly unhappy, everlastingly in conflict.

So to come to the point: Why do human beings never change? This is an important question. Why do you who live in conflict, misery, confusion, uncertainty, quarrelling with your wife, with your husband, with all that is going on in the family, accept it, live with it? Why? You understand my question? Is it because we are so accustomed to a particular pattern of thought, to a particular pattern of living that we are incapable of breaking that pattern? Is it laziness, is it fear of the unknown, accepting "what is" rather than moving out of "what is"? Is it that our brains have become so dull because of our education? You are all B.A.'s, M.A.'s, Ph.D.'s, and all the rest of it; is your education conditioning you to become an engineer for the rest of your life so that you are incapable of thinking of anything except building bridges, railways? Is our education destroying humanity?

Please, inquire into all this for God's sake! What will change man, which is, what will change your relationship with another? You understand? That is the basic question. We are all concerned with the changing of society, the ugliness, the brutality, the horror that is going on and we never ask or demand why each one of us doesn't change, change in our relationship.

So what is our relationship? What is your relationship with your wife, with your sister, with your daughter, with your husband, whatever it is? What is your relationship? Come on. Is that relationship based on egotistic pursuit, each one wanting his own particular way? You understand all this? So we have to inquire very carefully, and of course sceptically, into what is relationship. If we don't understand relationship we will never bring about the necessary revolution in society.

So what is relationship? Are we ever related to each other at all? You may have a wife, or a girlfriend, which is the modern fancy. You may have a husband or you may have several girls or ladies, but what is the basis of that relationship? Is it merely pleasure, sexual, is it merely a sense of comfort, convenience, social contact? Please inquire into all this. Do we dare to look into that relationship? Are we frightened to look into it? You understand my question? Are we frightened to look into our relationship—wife, daughter, girlfriend, husband, the whole structure of relationship in the family? Shouldn't we find out for ourselves what is the truth of relationship? So let us inquire; please don't accept what the speaker is saying. That would be too absurd, that would have no validity. It will have no significance in your life if you merely say, "Yes, somebody said that." But if you look into it, if you go into the question of relationship and observe it without any direction, without any motive, just observe it, what is it? First look at what is actually going on. Is it sexual pleasure or pleasure in companionship, pleasure of having someone with whom you can talk, bully, quarrel, or worship, adore? In that relationship, is there any love, or is that word, that feeling totally absent? And in this relationship with another you have an image of her and she has an image about you. Right? The relationship is between these two images that thought has created. I wonder if you see all this for yourself. I may have a wife or a husband. We have lived with each other for a number of years and I have built an image about her, a sexual image, the image of comfort, encouragement, somebody on whom I can rely, who will bear my children, and she has an image about me. I am not married, don't worry. Thank God! You laugh, but you don't see the tragedy of all this.

So what is your actual relationship? You have none. Right? You may have a house, a wife, children. You go to the office every day from nine to five or six o'clock for the next fifty years, come home, bed, quarrels, no time for anything except for money. If you are seeking power, position, status, that is your life—conflict—and you call that relationship. Right? Don't agree. See the fact and see if that image building can stop. You understand? Because most of us live with images, about ourselves and about others. The image of the politician, the image of the scientist, the image of the guru, the images made by the mind and by the hand, we live with images. The images become all-important, not living.

The question is whether the machinery that creates the image can come to an end. You follow what I am saying? Please come with me. We are taking the journey together. You are not being hypnotized by the speaker so please don't go to sleep. We are together walking the road, a very tortuous road, very complex road, with many turnings, dangerous bends, and together we have to understand a way of living that may be totally different, to have a society that is different and that society can only be different if you as a human being are different. It is a simple equation. So can we live without a single image? You have an image about yourself as a lawyer, as an engineer, as a saint, as a guru, as a follower, you have an image about yourself. Why? Is there security in that image? Because our mind, our brain is always searching for security, and you think there is security in a concept, in a belief, until somebody comes around and shakes it.

So is there security in the image that you have built about yourself? Because there is no security in a living thing, in a moving, active thing, but we think there is security in the image that we have created. You know, we think there is tremendous security in knowledge. If you are a professor, if you are a teacher, if you are a guru, if you are some kind of careerist, you have certain knowledge. That knowledge gives you a job, a skill, and in that you think there is great security. You have never questioned what knowledge is, knowledge apart from technological knowledge. Knowledge is invariably incomplete. You cannot have *complete* knowledge about anything. That is a fact. So knowledge is always in the shadow of ignorance. Just swallow that! It is always within the shadow of ignorance. So any action born out of knowledge must be incomplete. Therefore, being incomplete, it must invariably bring conflict. So the knowledge that you have about another in your relationship is incomplete, and therefore any action based on that knowledge, which is the image that you have about another, must bring about conflict. This is obvious. Is there a relationship that is not based on knowledge? That is, I know you as my wife, I have lived with you for twenty years and I know all about you, which is nonsense of course. But the knowledge I have is the image about you that thought has built. Do you understand all this?

The machinery that is the movement of thought in relationship creates the image and therefore division. Where there is division there must be conflict: between the Hindu and the Muslim, between India and Pakistan, the Arab and the Jew, the Socialist and the Catholic. Is it possible to end conflict in relationship? Inquire with me into the possibility of the complete ending of conflict. Let us inquire into why humanity, you, a human being who are the rest of mankind, why you live in conflict in your relationship. Conflict must exist where there is division. Right? That is the law and if you see the fact that you are not an individual, but the rest of mankind—including your wife whose face you have looked at for the last twenty years and got bored with—can conflict end? That is, why does thought enter into relationship? You see the point? Thought invariably divides, thought invariably creates the image: you and the other. Why does thought enter into relationship? Which means is thought love? Is thought desire, is thought pleasure in relationship?

We are asking why thought enters into relationship at all. Please go into it, inquire into it. Is not thought dividing us, you as a Hindu, I as a Muslim, I as a Communist, you as a Socialist? You know all that stuff. And especially in our relationship, why should thought enter at all? Please ask this question, not superficially, not merely verbally or as an abstract idea that you are going to examine, but why should thought enter into my relationship with another? What place has thought apart from the technological world? You understand my question? In the technological world I need thought to build a computer, to build a robot; to build anything, a chair, to plant a tree, I need thought. To learn a language I need thought. But why should thought enter into our relationship? Please look at it! Is it because it has created the image about another, as it has created the image about oneself and that image becomes more important than actual relationship? Is it that we like to live in illusion and not with actuality? Is actuality so unpleasant that we are unwilling to look at it?

So can you look at your daily relationship with your wife, with your boss? In that relationship, you as a self-centred entity become all-important and therefore there must inevitably be conflict. And can you look at your wife, at your husband, and not let the word interfere? The word is the thought—you understand?—the word is the symbol. When you say, "my wife," see what you have done. The word has become important. In that word there is this whole structure of possession, domination, attachment, and where there is attachment there must be corruption.

You listen to all this. Does this listening bring about an abstraction called an idea, or in the very act of listening do you see the truth of it? Which is actually going on in your brain: seeing the actual truth, or listening and making an abstraction of it into an idea and therefore the idea becomes all-important and not the fact? Are you actually observing what is the fact and can you—this is important, if I may point out—can you remain with the fact without any movement of thought? If I have created an image about myself, sitting on the platform with a large audience, with a reputation, the worldly blah-blah that I have written books, been praised, insulted, all that, that image can be trodden on, can be hurt. Somebody comes along and tells me, "My dear chap, you are very small compared to somebody else," and I get hurt because the image is hurt. If I have no image about myself at all—which is a fact with me—nobody can tread on it. Therefore a relationship with such a person is not based on thought and there is a relationship of an entirely different kind. That is for the speaker and it is not important. What is important is you in your relationship. Can you see the fact and remain with the fact, not find excuses, justifying it, suppressing it and running away from it, but actually remain with the fact that you are an image, which is the factor that brings conflict with another?

If you do so remain solidly, without any movement, then that energy which has been dissipated through suppression dissolves the fact. Do it and test it out, and you will see you then have a totally different kind of relationship with another and therefore a different society in which this terrible concept of an individual with his own pursuits, his shoddy ambition, and all the rest of it, comes to an end. You live totally differently. That means you live with love. I am afraid in this country and other countries that word has lost its meaning, but without that beauty of love, relationship becomes a horror.

From Commentaries on Living Second Series: *Conformity and Freedom*

To LIVE ALONE needs great intelligence; to live alone and yet be pliable is arduous. To live alone, without the walls of self-enclosing gratifications, needs extreme alertness; for a solitary life encourages sluggishness, habits that are comforting and hard to break. A single life encourages isolation, and only the wise can live alone without harm to themselves and to others. Wisdom is alone, but a lonely path does not lead to wisdom. Isolation is death, and wisdom is not found in withdrawal. There is no path to wisdom, for all paths are separative, exclusive. In their very nature, paths can only lead to isolation, though these isolations are called unity, the whole, the one, and so on. A path is an exclusive process; the means is exclusive, and the end is as the means. The means is not separate from the goal, the "what should be." Wisdom comes with the understanding of one's relationship with the field, with the passer-by, with the fleeting thought. To withdraw, to isolate oneself in order to find, is to put an end to discovery. Relationship leads to an aloneness that is not of isolation. There must be an aloneness, not of the enclosing mind, but of freedom. The complete is the alone, and incompleteness seeks the way of isolation.

Bombay, 24 January 1982

WE WANT TO change society. The Communists have tried it, there have been physical revolutions, always physical, shedding a lot of blood and so on. We all want to change society because it is corrupt, immoral, without any sense of human contact, and you cannot possibly change it unless our relationship with each other is completely and radically changed. That is very obvious. But we always want to change the outer without changing the inner structure of the human mind. We are together examining, looking, being sensitive, so as to be aware of what we are doing. This is a serious conversation, not something intellectual or emotional. A very serious man is a religious man. We are seriously considering human relationship. In human relationship there is conflict, pain, misery, and there is also so-called pleasure, and we are going to look at all these problems and whether it is possible radically to change a relationship in which there is hardly any love.

We are asking what relationship is. What does it mean to be related to another? Please, the speaker is asking the question, but we are thinking together about it. Now human relationship has become a problem. The meaning of that word *problem* is to have something thrown at you; it is a challenge, something flung at you, something that you have to face, something that you have to understand. And a challenge needs a right approach. So we have to understand what our approach is to a problem. There is this problem of human relationship, which is a problem in everybody's life; whether you are aware of it or not, it is there. How do you approach this problem? You understand my question? The problem exists. How do you come to it; with what mind, with what motive? How do you come closely into contact with the problem? Is the problem different from the observer who is examining the problem? You are following all this? Probably most of you will find this rather difficult because you have not thought about all these matters at all, so please be patient and let's go into it.

Suppose I have a problem. How do I look at it, how do I examine it, what is my response to it? So the problem is not important but how you approach it. Is that clear? Am I afraid of the problem? Or do I want to run away from it, or suppress it, or rationalize it? Or do I have a motive that I must find an answer to it? So I approach the problem with all my confusion, my uncertainty, my fear. We have to find out what your approach is, how you come to it. What is your motive? Your motive is to resolve it, if you are aware of that problem at all. You want to resolve it because it is painful. If the problem is most pleasurable it is not a problem. But when the problem becomes painful, confusing, bringing about insecurity, then you have to look at it, investigate it. So what is important is how you approach the problem.

How do you listen to what he is saying? What is your reception of it? Of course, you hear it through the sensory ear. You understand English and the speaker is speaking that language, you understand the word you hear through the sensory ear, but also there is hearing beyond the word, beyond the verbal interpretation. To listen so that you immediately understand what he is talking about is the art of listening. So we are asking now: How do you approach the problem? Your approach will dictate or resolve the problem, so find out how you approach any problem. It is very simple if it is a scientific problem, you approach it with all the knowledge you have and try to discover further information—about matter, about the atom, and so on. If you have a problem, do you approach it with all the past knowledge, with all the past remembrances, or do you approach the problem as though for the first time? Do you understand my question? Are you following?

Let's approach it differently. What actually is our relationship between man and woman? Apart from sexual relationship, is there any relationship at all? Or is each one going separately, in their own way, never meeting, except sexually? Like two railway lines never meeting, that is our relationship, is it not? So our relationship is merely sensory relationship, sexual relationship, and the relationship between each other is based on the images we have built about each other. Are you aware of all this? What actually is your relationship with another? Or do you have no relationship at all except sexual? If you have no relationship with each other, which I am afraid is the fact, then what is your life? Life *is* relationship. Without relationship you cannot exist. But we have reduced that relationship to mere sensory responses. I wonder if one is aware of this complexity of relationship. You cannot escape from it by becoming a hermit, a sannyasi, a monk; you cannot escape from having human relationship.

So we must examine very closely why human beings have lost not only relationship with nature but also with each other. You understand? Why? As we have said, merely seeking the cause will not bring about the resolution of the problem. You may find the cause, I will show you the cause, but the understanding of the cause, the examination of the cause, will not solve the problem. I know for example that we are selfish, totally self-centred, and we are self-centred because it is our habit, it is tradition, it is our religious upbringing: "You are a separate soul, you must seek your own salvation," and so on. This emphasis on being selfish, self-centred, through education, through pressure, has existed from time immeasurable. That is the cause of all this misery. We understand that intellectually, but discovering the cause does not make us less selfish. So we have said that what is important is not the analytical process of discovering the cause but remaining with the problem, which is that we are selfish. That is a fact, and therefore there is no relationship with each other. Each goes his own way. Divorces are multiplying, in Europe and in

America, and it is also coming here in India more and more; when women can earn their own livelihood, they walk out on men. So gradually there is a world in which hardly any relationship with each other exists. So we become very callous, self-centred, pursuing our own way. That is, our way is to become something, become more rich, become the chief executive, or become the high priest, the archbishop, and so on. There is all the struggle to become something, which is essentially selfish.

Now you have heard this, which we all know. When you hear such a statement what is your reaction to it? Do you accept it and say, "Yes, what you say is absolutely so," and just let it go? Or do you hear it, see the truth of it, and remain with that truth so that it operates, without *your* operating, on selfishness? Do you understand what I am saying?

Let's look at it. Suppose I am selfish and I say I must not be selfish. That is, thought has brought about selfishness. It has structured selfishness. Then thought says, "I must not be selfish," so there is conflict between the fact and what thought wants it to be. Right? Come on, let's go into it. Suppose I am violent. We human beings are violent, suppose I am violent. That is a fact. That is so. But I invent non-violence, which is non-fact. Right? I am violent; I do not know how to deal with it, what to do with it. I either indulge in it or try to understand it, try to go into it. And I think it will help me if I have the idea of non-violence, which this country has been preaching endlessly without any result. So conflict arises between "what is" and "what should be." The "what is" is fact, the "what should be" is non-factual. So can we drop the non-factual, the ideal, the "what should be" and only be concerned with "what is," which is violence? Right? That is a problem. You have the human problem: we want peace but yet we are violent. So the fact is we are violent. How do you approach that fact? How do you look at that fact? What is your intention when you look at that fact? Either you want to suppress it or run away from it, or transcend it, which means that you are not really then facing the fact; you are trying to escape from it. You are following all this? So we are saying remain with the fact, without translating the fact, without trying to run away from the fact. Look at it, be with it. When you are with it you give all your attention to it; but when you say, "I must transcend it," "I must escape from it," "I must pursue non-violence," you are wasting your energy. You are following all this? Therefore we are saying, remain with that fact which you call violence. Understand it, learn all about it. And you can only learn by watching. Right?

Now just a minute, there is a difference between learning and memorizing. All of us have been trained to memorize, which is not the same as learning. Learning is to observe and let what you observe tell its story.

So we are asking: What is our human relationship? If you are married, or if you have a girlfriend, or whatever you have, how do you look at her, or him? What is your reaction when you look at your husband, or wife? Or are you totally indifferent? Or do you say, "I have responsibility towards her and my children"? You are following all this? What is your inward true response? Are you going your way and she is going her way, so you never meet, because you are ambitious, competitive, wanting more money, a better job, and so on, and so on, and she also has her own ambitions, her own ideals. There is no relationship when two people are running parallel. You understand this? Of course! It is so simple when you look at it.

So then what is a relationship in which there is only sexual pleasure, and is pleasure love? I am asking you a question. Please find out. Is love sexual pleasure? Is pleasure love? We won't go into the question of what love is. That requires a great deal of understanding, great sensitivity, appreciation of nature as beauty, beauty of form, beauty of a face, beauty of the sky. And without all that sensitive appreciation of nature you will never find out what love is. But if you have reduced life, the living in relationship, to sexual pleasure, and each person pursuing his own way, then you will have tremendous conflict, insupportable rebellion, which is going on in our life between man and woman.

So in examining our relationship with each other, intimate or not, one begins to understand, or learn, and find out whether it is possible to live together as two people, man, woman, without any conflict whatsoever. Being sensitive to each other and having no conflict whatsoever in that relationship, is that possible? Because our life, our daily continuous life, day after day is a series of conflicts, endless conflicts until we die. We have never known a life without a single moment of conflict; is this conflict necessary in relationship? That is, as long as you have an image of her, and she has an image about you, there must be conflict. Right? You build an image about her, or she about you, through habit, through quarrels, through nagging, through encouraging. You are supporting each other through words, through flattery, through insult, all that is building an image about her, and she about you. This is what we are doing. Right, sirs? Now, is it possible to live with another person never having an image about each other? Please learn about it! That is, I have an image about my wife—I am not married but suppose I have an image about my wife. (Laughter) Why do you laugh when I say I am not married? Why do you laugh? Are you laughing because I am a lucky man? Are you laughing because to you laughter is a means of escaping from the fact? Please, we are talking about very, very serious things, about life, about our daily living. Don't pass it off by laughing. We have to face this terrible existence in which there is no happiness, no love.

You see the speaker is deeply concerned to bring about a transformation of the human mind. He is concerned. He feels it is a tremendous responsibility and therefore he is talking about it. As we are living now, in utter selfishness, callous, indifferent, brutal, insensitive, we are destroying each other. And we are asking: Is it possible to live without a single conflict in our relationship? I say, the speaker says, it is possible, completely possible. Although he is not married, the speaker has lived with a great many people, in their houses, friends and so on, without building an image about anybody. You know what that requires? A very quick mind, not a mind that is clogged with knowledge, clogged with remembrances, clogged with experiences, but a mind that is very quick, alert, watchful. When you are watchful of what is happening around you, in the street, when you get into a bus, or when you get into a train, an airplane, or when you are walking along the street, to watch, to look, be sensitive to everything that is happening around you, then you become very sensitive to your relationship. Is it possible to live a life in which there is no conflict whatsoever?

First of all, understand the question, the beauty of that question: to live a life, not ideally, not as an ideal that you must achieve, but the fact of whether you can live a life without a single conflict. The question itself has great beauty in it. You put that question because you are sensitive, you are aware of this enormous conflict between human beings, which ends in war, in divorce, in total neglect of each other, callousness, and all that. But if you put to yourself the question whether you can live a life in which struggle, conflict, can ever end, if you put that question seriously to yourself, then that question will begin to evolve. The question itself will stir up a great many problems and you have to face those problems. And in facing them there must be no motive, there must be no struggle to understand it. Look at it.

Have you ever been to museums, some of you? You have, I am sure. Have you ever looked at a picture, not comparing a picture by Rembrandt with modern art, but just looking at one picture without comparing it with other pictures? Have you ever done it, just remained with that one picture, sat in front of it and looked at it? Then the picture will tell you its story, what the artist wanted you to understand. But if you approach that picture by comparing it with one by somebody else, then you are not looking at it.

Similarly, you are the story of mankind. In you is the residue of all man's endeavour, all man's suffering, his anxiety. Look! You as a human being are not alone, you are like the rest of mankind: you suffer, you have pain, you are seeking security, are uncertain, confused, in agony, and so is the man in Europe, or in America, or in Russia, or in China. So there is a continuity of human suffering of which you are. You are the rest of mankind. You *are* mankind. So you are not alone, you are not in your consciousness something separate, you are the rest of mankind. You are not an individual. You are the whole of humanity, because humanity has gone through endless pain, immeasurable sorrow, with occasional flares of joy and love. You are that. So you have to understand that. And the story of mankind is you. You have to learn how to read the book of mankind, which is yourself. Understand all this! You are the story of mankind and you have to read that book. Either you read it page by page, which is to know all the content of suffering, pain, joy, pleasure, the terrible anxiety and agony, or you skip, you say, "I know all about it." Or by reading the first chapter you have understood the whole book.

Knowing oneself, which is self-knowing, is important in relationship. If you don't know yourself, what you are, all your troubles, your anxieties, your uncertainties, desire for security, if you don't understand all that, how can you understand your wife or your husband? They will remain two separate entities. So relationship means not only physical contact, which is sexual, but having no image about each other. Therefore there is immediate sensitive relationship in which there is love. Love is not remembrance. Love is not the picture that thought creates about another. That is not love. Love is not pleasure. I wonder if you understand all this?

So it is important to understand the nature and the structure of relationship. To change this corrupt society you must change yourself radically. We are concerned about that only: to bring about a mutation in the very mind, in the very cells of the brain. The speaker has discussed this problem with scientists, brain specialists, whether the brain, which has been conditioned through time to function within the area of knowledge, whether that brain can radically be changed; and it can radically be changed when there is a total insight into the whole human problem. Insight is not remembrance. I won't go into it now because it is too complex. So please understand what our conversation is about, which is our relationship with each other. As two friends walking along a beautiful lane full of trees and birds, and numberless shadows, we are investigating the nature of the brain, the mind, nature of our heart, whether in that structure there can be total transformation so that we are different human beings, with different minds, with compassion.

So please do become serious sometime, not just for this moment, but be serious through life. To be really profoundly serious is to be religious; not the religion of going to temples, church services, and all that kind of stuff, that is not religion. The man who is diligent in his seriousness, that man is a truly religious man.

Sources and Acknowledgments

From the Authentic Report of the fourth public talk 16 June 1940 at Ojai in *Collected Works of J. Krishnamurti* copyright © 1991 Krishnamurti Foundation of America.

From the transcript of the third public question and answer meeting 31 July 1981 at Saanen copyright © 1992 Krishnamurti Foundation Trust, Ltd.

From the Verbatim Report of the seventh public talk 15 August 1948 in Bangalore in *Collected Works of J. Krishnamurti* copyright © 1991 Krishnamurti Foundation of America.

From the Verbatim Report of the second public talk 17 July 1949 at Ojai in *Collected Works of J. Krishnamurti* copyright © 1991 Krishnamurti Foundation of America.

From the Verbatim Report of the third public talk 4 December 1949 in Rajahmundry in *Collected Works of J. Krishnamurti* copyright © 1991 Krishnamurti Foundation of America.

From the Verbatim Report of the first public talk 25 December 1949 in Colombo in *Collected Works of J. Krishnamurti* copyright © 1991 Krishnamurti Foundation of America.

From the Verbatim Report of the first radio talk 28 December 1949 in Colombo in *Collected Works of J. Krishnamurti* copyright © 1991 Krishnamurti Foundation of America.

From the Verbatim Report of the second public talk 1 January 1950 in Colombo in *Collected Works of J. Krishnamurti* copyright © 1991 Krishnamurti Foundation of America.

From the Verbatim Report of the third public talk 8 January 1950 in Colombo in *Collected Works of J. Krishnamurti* copyright © 1991 Krishnamurti Foundation of America.